Introduction

by

Donald Murray

During the 1930's when my father wrote his memories of his WW1 military service, he chose to write them in Esperanto. During the 1920's he had learnt Esperanto and had become an enthusiastic member of the London Esperanto community. His Esperanto narratives were found amongst his personal documents and translations have been assemble into this book.

His Civil Service career continued until his retirement in 1957, when he was awarded an O.B.E. Following his retirement he pursued a number of Esperanto activities. He was a member and for some years was president of the British branch of KELI (League of Christian Esperantists International). He also taught Esperanto in a Secondary Modern school in Southend-on-Sea, as well as hosting a small Esperanto club in Southend.

Acknowlegments to Trustees of the Regimental Museum for permission

to use the Regimental Emblem

ISBN: 9781549910029

[2nd edition]

My Adventures in the Great War
1915 to 1919
by
Robert Murray

Contents

Chapter I - Enlistment and Training p.3

Chapter II - France p.12

Chapter III - Salonica p.42

Chapter IV - Egypt and Palestine p.84

Postscript   p.130

Appendices:-

Timeline p.133

About the Kilt   p.142

Concert Programme p.143

The Lewis Gun p.146

Chapter I

Enlistment and Training

When the Great War started I was a 16-year-old young man who, seven months before, began to earn his wages as junior clerk in the government's Patent Office. Two years prior to this date I had lost my mother and became a fervent Christian. I thought that the war was not justifiable because it was against the peaceful ideals of Christ. I thought that, even if the fighting would last until the time when I should become a soldier, I would not go as a combatant. However, during the following months, I heard the clergy say that ours is God's battle and they blessed our troops and, little by little, my view changed. After the Christmas time of 1914, I had a strong desire to be enrolled in the army, especially when I heard that my friend, although only 17 years old, had become a soldier. The youngest age for a soldier was 19 years, but I was not bothered about that because I was a strong young man and tall for my age. However, I decided to wait a bit, because in February, I had to take an examination to obtain a permanent position in the civil service. After I'd taken the exam I didn't wait to hear the result, I asked permission from the office, and, having got it, I immediately visited the recruitment-office to enlist as a private soldier. I told the necessary lie about my age; I said 19 years instead of 17; passed the medical tests and then I swore to serve my king faithfully, and from then I was a soldier. For several days I slept at home and paraded daily for physical training and military training. My regiment was the 14th London Regiment (London Scottish) and consisted of Scots or children of Scots living in London.

I have to explain that there were many Scots in London and they belonged to all sorts of groups, clubs, and e.t.c, where they met fellow Scots or their children. It was like that in my regiment. Perhaps a brief description of the regiment would be of interest. In fact the London Regiment was really two divisions, consisting of 24 infantry regiments and others of cavalry and artillery, engineers, etc. The regiments 13 to 24 were in the second division, while the regiments 1a through 12a is the first division. Some of the regiments were "regular" soldiers (professional soldiers), but most of them were voluntary soldiers (Territorials). Because of this, the first division went France separately, along with other divisions of professional soldiers. Initially some of the regiments in the second division were in France separately in August 1914, and among them was my regiment, the London Scottish. Later after some heroic episodes, they joined with the rest of the division and were called the 47a Division. In 1915 when I enrolled in the second battalion of the London Scottish, they sent men from my battalion to replace the dead and wounded in the first battalion, in the 47a Division. Later on we ceased to send men to France and they formed us into the 60th (London) Division. From that time we began to prepare to go overseas. In this division of 12 regiments, there were three brigades, 179a. 180a and 181a. My brigade was the 179a and was called the "Grey Brigade", because the traditional uniform was mostly grey. The regiments were very friendly and at the same time very competitive and proud of their own regiments traditions. The regiments were 13th Regiment (Kensington), 14th (London Scottish), 15th (Civil Service) and the 16th Regiment (Westminsters). In every battalion were four companies, each with 200 men and also 200 other men for the office, food, transport, signals, ambulance, etc. In each company were 4 platoons and in each platoon there were 4 sections. Now you understand a little about the kind of army I was in. In territorials (voluntary) regiments the soldiers and officers come from the same living conditions and homes, and because of this the severe discipline, which is typically found in the army, was not found in our regiments.

On the 1st of March, I received my uniform and cut the link with civilian life. My uniform would be of interest to you because it included traditional Scottish clothing – the kilt. The kilt is a multi-pleated skirt which reaches the knees which were bare [sf - p.130 & p.142]. The rest of the uniform

4

was, more or less, ordinary male clothing, except for the hat, which is a 'Glengarry' worn on one side of the head [sf- p.132]. I was a proud young man when on the 9th of March, 1915, we marched through the streets of London to the station to go to Dorking to join up with my regiment, where they were preparing themselves to fight. Our first battalion had already gone to France in the early days of the war, and they had sent soldiers from the second battalion to fill the ranks after the losses from death and injury. I soon became accustomed to military life because I was young and strong and because it was a good adventure. I lived with five companions in a furniture room above a shop in the village and we slept on the floor. We were only in this town for three weeks, but we became famous for part of our daily routine - the daily change of the guard. The change of the guard is a ceremonial affair led by the adjutant of the regiment. He was a good soldier but quite impatient. The members of the guard most of the time were recruits, who are not well acquainted with the ceremony or the ceremonial movements. Therefore, you can imagine how the adjutant became angry, jumped up and down on his horse, screamed and cursed the poor guardsmen. That happened on the street, in front of the regimental office, and soon the villagers came every evening to see the funny sight. For those who watched it was good fun - for the soldiers it was depressing experience. I am glad to say that I did not have to live through such a humiliating experience. By the time I was first on guard duty, I was an adequately trained soldier.

We left Dorking 29th March to go by train to Watford - a town 17 miles north of London. There we stayed two months and the soldiers lived in the houses with the townspeople. My friend and I stayed with a kindly family, with whom we became good friends. The military training continued, but they also arranged good sporting activities. There was the football competition between battalions of the brigade. After hectic matches, our regiment won the "cup" as the champions. What a day that was! On the playing field, after the game, we danced and shouted while the bagpipers played Scottish victory tunes. Then we formed ranks and marched through the town. At the front the bagpipers were playing marching music, following behind were the soldiers with the

5

"cup" high in the air on a long pole, and they were followed by most of the regiment. We went through the town again and we were singing about the victory. In the evening we prepared a concert in a large hall. The officers announced that "you can drink beer for free" (paid for by the officers) and we enjoyed ourselves there with a song, a joke and a chorus till two in the morning. So our stay at Watford was spent happily and passed quickly.

On the 17th May we set out from Watford to go to Saffron Walden, a small town in the county of Essex. We walked there, taking four days. The first day we walked to the town of Hatfield, where we spent the night in the stables of Hatfield House, the mansion of Lord Salisbury. The next day we went to Ware. This walk was not long and we spent the afternoon with a visit to the cinema, where we saw a film, called "WAR IS HELL". This was propaganda film against Germans soldiers and suggested that the officers mostly thought of wine and women, and less about war.

On the 19th, we continued our journey as far as Bishops Stortford, and on the 20th we got to Saffron Walden. My company lived for a few days in the school, and later at the city hall. Here I slept under a bench in the gallery. It was a pretty comfortable, but but one night I cursed the place a lot, because, waking suddenly, I immediately sat up and banged my head against the seat.

On the 28th of May, I went with my friends to a nearby village, Welwyn, to practice the use of the rifle. Welwyn was a very good village and there in a comfortable house we spent a very good week. After our return to Saffron Walden, we were in camp and it was the first time I had slept in a tent. From time to time during the summer, small parties of the regiment left us to go to France. Whenever this happened, everyone had volunteered to go. In September 1915, I got a pass with a free ticket to Scotland, and I took the opportunity to visit my relatives in Golspie, a small village in northern Scotland. Returning, I visited Invergordon and Edinburgh where I had relatives. At the end of September, we began to make manoeuvers across the country, as by this time, the farmers had harvested their crops. One day, we attacked the village of

Littlebury; then we walked in one day to Stebbing and the next day made a large attack against Braintree. During these activities, we had to sleep in the open air, and we gradually acquired the art of soldiering. I do not know why; whether it was because we were successful or unsuccessful, but we had to repeat this attack against Braintree three times.

On the 25th of October, we left Saffron Walden, and walked to Bishops Stortford, where I found an excellent lodging with a poor family, of which three sons have fought in France. Unfortunately, I did not stay there long, for my company had to go to Hertford for special duty. The 8th of November brought a new experience for me, because they sent us to Stanstead to learn something about grenades - hand grenades. This was an interesting time for us as we had only heard of hand grenades and we had a lot to learn. During one of these lessons, I saw the officer-in-charge receive the greatest shock of his life when he stood in place, which was according to his opinion sufficiently safe, a fragment, of one of the bombs thrown into a trench, hit his hat. He did not stay there long. This was one of the very rare occasions when I saw the officer-in charge in a dangerous place. I successfully completed the course, and this allowed me wear the badge of an expert bomber on my arm, which made me very proud. On the 24th of November I was again in Hertford, and on the 28th, we went back to Bishops Stortford, where I went into new lodgings. These new lodgings was not with a poor family; but what a difference!! In the poor home, I and a comrade were given an all-out welcome. But in this house, of a rich person, what did we find? The lady owner met us at the door and said that we always have to come in through the side door. In the room where we slept, there were no comforts. On the wall the only ornament was a poster that informed us that our King needs us! She did her best to get rid of us because of the inconvenience, and we would gladly have gone if we could.

In December, I attended a second bomb course at Stanstead. That Christmas evening, I waited in the cold on guard against any hostile activities. That was neither fun nor enjoyable, but I would have been no luckier if I had remained in the lodgings. There was another regiment in Bishops

Stortford, and we and they arranged the Christmas festivities. The Scots always celebrate New Year rather than Christmas, and this gave the regiments the opportunity to work together on the matter. So, the other regiment celebrated the Christmas night, and our non-commissioned officers were to serve them at the table. Then, on the final evening of the year, we had an excellent evening party and concert, etc., and the other regiment helped us with these.

At the end of January, 1916, we were brought together with the other regiments of the division to be part of a new army to go to France in the following summer. After that we did not send any more parties to the 1st Battalion in France, but in London they formed a 3rd battalion from which to send men to the 1st Battalion and us. To finish our military training, they sent us to the town of Warminster, next to the famous Salisbury Plain. We left London on January 21 by train and walked from the station in Warminster to a camp near a village called Sutton Veny (No. 9 Camp). Around Warminster were gathered the whole of the division to which our regiment belonged, and the life changed somewhat to make it more like normal military life. Before then, I had had a variety of lodgings - for example in a private house, where I and a friend lived with the family; in an empty shop with six other friends; in a room in a school; in a gallery; in a tent in camp; and so on. But now we lived in long wooden huts - 30 in each hut. Each of the regiments, in the division, was in its own camp, and these stretched out one after the other. Before we went to Salisbury Plain, I had learnt something about first aid and signaling, and I also earned the badge of a bomber. I had always tried to become a member of any class to learn any special skills [i.e. map reading], because such learning was usually easier and not as boring as the regular training. Whilst in Warminster, the division undertook strenuous exercises involving long marches, night-manoeuvers, trench-making, etc. Often late at night in Warminster, parties of soldiers from various regiments would try to hire one of the few taxis to get back to camp quickly and had battles on the streets about it, and often when the two parties of soldiers were fighting for a taxi, a third party would come out and engage the taxi, and go off in it before the fighters were aware of what had happened.

One February weekend, there was a heavy fall of snow and most of us stayed in the huts during the Saturday afternoon, some read, others wrote letters, and some even slept. Suddenly the door of the hut opened and many snowballs were thrown in. For several minutes we were amazed, but we realised that some soldiers from a nearby camp had attacked us. Our battle cry rang out through the camp, and soon our men were gathered to withstand their attack. The battle continued for two hours and finally we drove the attackers away and went to their camp, where we threw snow into their huts and at the same time took some souvenirs. We were covered by snow, but nothing serious had happened and we enjoyed the sport. The following Sunday, we had prepared to attack another regiment, and a second battle took place. After initial success, we were suddenly attacked from the side by another regiment and were completely surprised; and so had to flee rapidly in disorder.

About that time I was made one of the regiment chefs and learnt a new job. That was a pretty good job, and when I was a cook, I avoided a lot of severe manoeuvers. However, I did not like the job much and I got sent back to the company again as an ordinary soldier. By this time I had served for one year, and the captain put me with six others in a class to learn the duties of a corporal. I had no desire become a corporal, because I was only 18 years old (although I was officially 20 years old), and I thought I was too young to command men, one of whom was nearly enough old to be my father. So I asked that they put me in the class to learn about machine-guns, and because that section of the company was very dangerous, I obtained that permission and again I was a student to become a specialist. That happened in March shortly after the arrival of the first machine-guns of this type (Lewis Guns) [sf p.146]. It was a light weapon and could fire very rapidly, and as such, it was very useful for trench warfare. I very much enjoyed the instruction, and very soon became an expert.

On 24 April, we went to a nearby camp to another village called Longbridge Deverill. We did not stay there long in peace, because at the time there was the emergency of the

9

rebellion in Ireland against England, and on the 28th of April, our brigade was ordered to go there to fight against the insurgents. Initially, the entire division had to go. But out of the total division, my company alone remained in England to guard the quantities of equipment that had been left in the camps. Those who went had many adventures. Some of the adventures were very funny, because of the fact that they did not know who was friendly amongst the population of the country. In fact, many of the Irish highly disapproved of the rebellion, and because of this, it was quite quickly suppressed, and after one month, our comrades were able to come back and leave the final suppression of the rebellion to local soldiers.

(They had landed at Port Nolloth, Queenstown, walked up to Forty Island; the battalion headquarters were at Trallee).

Our military training ended in May, and on the 27th of May, our King George Vth came to Warminster to inspect us. A ceremonial inspection was something worth seeing. All soldiers were gathered on a hill behind the King, and then walked over to the left, turned twice to the right and then walked before past the King. We were the last but one regiment, and we watched the other ten, one after the other, march past. It really was a show very worth seeing.

After some days we were all able to go home to make our last farewells before going to France. I stayed at home six days and then after a dismal farewell to the family and to my Daisy, I returned to Salisbury Plain to set out on these unknown and dangerous adventures in a foreign country. What will happen? May be death? May be injury, whether there would be honour, or the shame of cowardice? I did not know nor really care, nor thought much about it as young blood ran through my veins.

Finally the much awaited day came. The goodbyes had been made; the final preparation done and all was in good order and then came the command "Forward to the station." There without shouting and rushing the whole regiment entrained as quietly as if they were going for a picnic. At

Southampton we went aboard the "Margate Belle" which pre-war was a pleasure boat, that sailed between London and Margate during the summer months. There were so many men aboard, that it was almost impossible to move from one part of the ship to another. I found myself a seat among some ropes on the deck. In the evening I began the journey and when the sun went down the shores of our beloved England went out of sight. What personal thoughts we had during this time! Were we ever likely to see these shores again? Will we have good or bad adventures in France? For me one of the most tormenting questions was - "will I be a coward in the face of the enemy"? My biggest fear was that maybe I would be a coward in dangerous circumstances? Because of such thoughts and the general excitement I could not sleep; later I could not sleep because of the cold, and finally I saw the green and red lights that announced our approach to Le Havre.

Chapter II

France

Then I fell asleep and again woke up in the morning sunshine beside the pier in Le Havre and there was an unpleasant sight of the 'consequences of the war'. Next to the pier was a hospital and on the balcony were some wounded who were suffering from severe wounds because they were covered by bandages. Wasn't that a dreary welcome to France? However, we could not think about this for long because the landing soon began. We walked to a camp not far from the port and after breakfast, returned to the pier and worked most of the day to disembark the regimental equipment. In the evening I was back in the camp and soon fell asleep from the fatigue of the journey. Early in the morning I got up and we soon found ourselves on the way to the station where we boarded a train and again set off to go 'somewhere'.

The station was called Gare de Marchandise and from there we travelled through the day. The sun had already started to go down when we passed through Rouen. Finally we stopped at some village. At 4 in the morning, we got out. It was raining hard and cold. It was noticed that the name of the station was Petit Houvain, so this is France! We walked, I do not know how many kilometres. The road seemed to be endless; probably due to our weariness. The first town that we came to was Buneville, where we breakfasted and then rested. Then we continued the journey to Averdoingt. There they dispersed us into various places to spend the night.

I found myself on a bed of straw in some stables. During the next day we walked further on, and the June weather was not too bad, I really enjoyed the adventure. On occasions we could hear the distant rumble of guns. Finally, on 25th June 1916, we were close enough to the battle line, that we had to rest by the road until evening to avoid showing the hostile aeroplanes that were many soldiers moving into the area. We sat by the road for some hours and watch the aeroplanes that patrolled over trenches. Suddenly there was a burst of machine gun fire and we saw enemy aeroplanes attacking ours. How exciting it was for us! How cleverly they manoeuvred in the air to enter into a good position to shoot at one of the opponents. Presently one of our aeroplanes landed behind us, and we assumed that the pilot was injured. Then more planes came from our side and the Germans had to leave because of the greater number of their opponents. When this battle was finished it was almost night and we started to walk on to the village Maroueil which we reached after two hours and were soon asleep in the soldier's huts. This village was behind the third defence line and there soldiers rested between their spells of duty in the trenches. During the night of the 26 - 27th of June I was suddenly awakened by something and then I heard a sharp sound, which gradually got louder and after some seconds there was very loud explosion which shook the building in which we were. Presently followed by another, and another and we began to think that it might be a German attack on the village because we do not know anything about where it was or how far away the German lines were.

However we were not in doubt for long, because a voice commanded us to follow him immediately and we went into "dugouts" (perhaps four metres below ground - where people sheltered during bombardment). Here we found other soldiers who have served in this place some weeks and they explained to us that "Jerri" (our name for the Germans) bombarded of the village at night, from time to time, and that during the bombardment everyone must shelter in the dugouts. Probably the enemy had somehow learned about our arrival (probably from the aeroplanes that we saw in the fight), because that night was more than a normal bombardment lasting more than two hours. Our hut was not damaged, and finally we went back to finish our rest.

The next day (June 27), we have received the order to prepare ourselves to go off 'somewhere' in the evening. With full equipment we left the village when the sun went down in the west, and walked for an hour (more or less) on the road until we reached a crossroads. We crossed the main road and soon entered a trench system which led us forward near the road which was too dangerous to walk along, because of the machine gun fire from the enemy. Walking in a trench system was a new experience for us and we did not like it much. It was a narrow path on 'duck boards' which were often under slimy water that often came over our boots – in this way we continued with curses. Then we began to get used to such a life but by that evening we were students who did not like the lesson. After an hour we came to a road that passed over the trench that we now left to go a bit to the right. Presently we stopped. We gradually proceeded until we came to the entrance of a shaft into which we went. By candle-light we went down, down, till then, when we were fifteen meters below the ground we were in a cave partially illuminated by candles. We received the order to lay down our back pack and go on in "fighting equipment" - that is with a gun, ammunition, bombs, water bottle and mess tins and a trenching tool. They ordered us to walk to the store where we got something to wear (denims). Then we learned that we were preparing to go to work beyond our front line, between our line and the German. This was the entrance to a large underground excavation that extended far under German trenches to a hill that was one of the strong points in their defence system. Our engineers, the 185th Tunnelling Co., RE, were preparing for a huge explosion under that hill to help our battle plans. We were those who had to carry the wood, powder, tools, etc. to the engineers. Presently we proceeded and the excitement continued. The trench in which we were was part of a large network of trenches and if you lost sight of the man in front of you, you seriously risked losing the way. Therefore, if the man in front hurried, everyone had to hurry, even though his shoulder was agonised by the wood or the barbed wire that they carried. I brought a bag of powder (gunpowder) and I have always wondered about what would happen if a bullet or piece of shrapnel hit the bag. Everything finally finishes, either for good or bad, and we soon received the order to stop. I was at the front of the party, and we were led into trench which they said was the front line. Think about my feelings! Here I am, finally in the trench with the enemy in front of me. The place about which I had often read and wanted to be. Hush! No talking out loud else someone might hear you and throw a grenade! During our progress the bullets and mortars went hissing over our heads, and from

14

time to time shrapnel landed beside us and really we did not know what was happening. We were in a dangerous place now, and we began to understand things a little better. From time to time a flare is shot into the air when a nervous lookout thought he heard some kind of enemy movement. Presently we went further ahead on a narrower trench and we found ourselves between the two front lines. From that trench we went into the entrance of the mine. We went underground through an inclined tunnel until we came to a small cavern in whose floor was a hole that led to the tunnel that went a fraction of a kilometre under the German line.

Our party formed a very long chain of people out of the mine, down in the trench across "No Man's Land" and through it to another part of the line. To begin with, things that we brought were passed from man to the next, and finally every item disappeared into the hole, where it was given to the working miners. Then they sent up to us bags of earth, which we passed from hand to hand along the human chain, and eventually we passed these along to the last man who emptied the bags which were then returned to the mine. This was done so as to conceal the entrance of this important mine. This work continued for a few hours and I felt very faint. At sunrise, we left the place and returned via the connecting trench to the big cave at Neuville St. Vaast. There the always welcome cup of tea was waiting for our return. We ate cakes, jam, drank the tea, then cleaned us as far as possible and finally fell asleep. During the day we could not do much, because it was dangerous to move much during daylight. So, by the day we slept, ate, and sometimes lay still on a beautiful grass in the fresh air. This was a special pleasure in contrast to the foul atmosphere of the cave. Below, there was no daylight, except in one place where there was the hole through which we passed various things up and down. The only lighting was candles! After the first night, we returned to the mine seven more times to work. The weather, which initially was beautiful and summery, suddenly changed. Warning clouds flew across the blue sky. After that more clouds and these clouds started to rain on us, which soon became a downpour. Of course the water collected in the trenches. At first it did not matter much, because there were drainage holes, like little 'fleas' in a corner of each part of the

15

trench, and the water flowed into them. Even now we could move easily in the main trenches because of the wooden walkways. In the smaller trenches the water was soon deep enough to wet everyone to above the knees. Also, the mud persistently stuck to our clothes. Then life, and especially the work, became very annoying and unpleasant. Dear reader, you can imagine the miserable state of unhappy people who have to wade twenty or thirty yards in a trench whose floor is a third of a meter below the water level. With a bag of earth on one's shoulder, the task of carrying becomes increasing very difficult. Finally, possibly some poor person stumbles, because of the slippery bottom of the trench, and falls and sits in the water. Oh yes, I'll never forget the week that we spent there during our first visit to the front line. One night, the enemy subjected us to the dubious pleasure of two hours' intense bombardment. We were ordered to leave the job and shelter wherever possible. I well remember the occasion. I and a comrade found a place in an underground dugout. But it was not far below ground. And ceaselessly the ground around us vibrated due to the shells exploding nearby. Also there were three comrades from a Scottish regiment, who were on duty in the line. In the pale light of a candle, light that vibrated with the ground and made strange shadows, and occasionally went out because of the gust of wind from a nearby exploding shell, in the uncertain light, I looked at the faces of the Scots to see if it was possible to guess whether they felt afraid. If they were afraid, they did not showed any sign. They were pale, but that was from fatigue, not fear. They looked young, not much more than boys, but compared to us they were veterans because they have already fought for seven months in France. We didn't talk a lot about it. When I realized that this was not a time to be afraid, I suddenly felt exhausted and soon fell asleep. A comrade woke me up and I immediately felt something strange. Oh yes, the ground no longer vibrated. The bombardment had ended not long before and we had to resume work. The Scotsmen had already gone back to their sentry duty.

The village of Neuville St. Vaast, which was near the cave, was a total ruin. It was probably situated at the intersection of roads and, when we first saw it, nothing remained but heaps of red bricks. Certainly there wasn't even one wall to show where any house had once stood. It was just a brick desert by the wayside. Next to the cave was a mortuary, where bodies of the dead lay waiting for a vehicle to take them to the cemetery. There for the first time I saw a war dead. He was a man who had received a bullet in the head as he crossed the road singing.

Well, such was the life we lived from the 27th of June until the 5th of July. We had worked to help miners tunnel a long way under the German lines to prepare for an explosion to remove the hill. The company was called the 185th Tunneling Co. R.E. (185th Tunneling Company, Royal Engineers), and they were all professional miners. One day, I noticed one of them who carried his gun with him, completely wrapped up in cloth so he could not use it. He explained that according to orders he had to carry it, and because of that he wrapped it up so that it did not get rusty. But, I said, how can you use it if you encounter an enemy? "Oh," he replied, "we do not meet Germans underground, and even if so, it would be easier to hit him with a shovel than to shoot him with a gun." During that this period, in addition to tea, our only food was canned beef (which we called "bully beef ") and biscuits. The battalion was guarded by Scottish soldiers, dressed kilts, of the regiment Gordons and Black Watch. I always felt safe, even in this dangerous place, when I saw those silent vigilant figures, who kept watch in the darkness.

The 5th of July, I went back with my comrades to Maroeiul, the village where the regiment was to be found. They ordered me to go to the machine gun section of the company, and I found new friends under Corporal Johnson. The next day we again went up by the now well-known way back as a battalion - but now not to work, but to help guard the trenches and learn a bit more about trench warfare.

On 9th July the reformed regiment left the line and walked to the village of Ecoivres for three days' rest. It had rained during our three days in the line and the trenches were waterlogged and our clothes all covered with mud. So, we had to spend much of our rest period getting rid of the mud. However, in the evening we were free to explore the town, but it was not much to see. One or two bars (typically french) where one could buy wine and food, and one or two young women who courageously remained to entertain those who desired it and would pay, and besides that there was nothing, except partially ruined buildings. I did not want female fun and so I with colleagues went into a bar to eat, drink and sing. The three days soon passed, and again we went up to the line where there was the constant thunder of various weapons. Early in the morning, the 13th of July, we replaced Regiment (7th Deeside Gordons) in the sector before Neuville St. Vaast. My machine gun section was in a forward position called Forges Gap, and there in front of the main line we were in a position very close to the German lines. When the Scots went away, I felt a bit doubtful about my ability to defend this place if the enemy should attack. But soon this feeling of apprehension went away and I felt that I should stay there and shoot until the departure of the enemy or of my life. We spent two hours on lookout and rested for four. During the four we had to take care of personal matters, the gun, grenades, etc.

At night, we stood up in order to get a better view; during the day we sat in front of a periscope – an arrangement of mirrors through which one could see a pretty broad section of the immediately adjacent front. But we almost never saw anything except the defence works of the Germans. We soon became accustomed to the situation and it became a bit boring during the day, but at night it was often more exciting.

When the Gordons left us, they did not go to the village, but remained in the support line, which is called Rawson Street. When on 16th July they again replaced us, we went into Rawson Street.

On the 19th of July, we went back to Forges Gap and the Gordons left the line completely and they left our regiment as the sole guardians of this section of the battle front.

The sector, in which we found ourselves and defended for nearly four months, was called the N sector, along with Neuville St. Vaast and extended 750 meters from north to the south. The front line, known for most of its length as Doublement, followed the line of some old farm lane. The trench line was deep, and well-built, and in it were the headquarters of three companies, who were in the line. From this line many small trenches passed, going towards the trenches of the Germans, where the front line was approximately 225 meters away. An important part of the system was the Paris Redoubt (fortress), a double circular trench, which was in front of Doublement. Along the right side of the line was the famous "Argyll" crater, the largest of its kind. We defended the western lip of the crater, while the Germans occupied the eastern. Between the two trench systems, "No Man's Land" was a labyrinth of disused trenches, barbed wire, and the permanent remains of a battlefield, where, not long ago there had been ferocious hand-to-hand fighting. Approximately 180 meters behind the front line, and running parallel, was the second line, which is called Rocade trench. Four hundred and fifty yards behind, in a low road were the reserve positions, where there were a number of main dugouts and smaller dugouts, called Sapper, Elbe and Vistula. From there to the rear were three long communication trenches, Claudot, Territorial and Victoire. One could, using the Territorial trench, walk from the village Maroeuil to the line, a distance of about four miles. In addition to these main trenches were many others less important, and the whole was part of that famous defense system, which the French called "The Labyrinth", for which, the French had so heroically and vigorously fought to capture in 1915 before the British became responsible for the sector.

The 51st Division which we had replaced was very weak in numbers, and because of this trenches and dugouts were not in a good state of repair, and so we had to begin a great deal of work immediately to improve them. At the same time, work was required for other reasons; such as repairing the damage done every day by the enemy shells. This time the line was comparatively quiet, because, due to a lack of troops our generals did not want to start an attack. Far to the south we could hear the continuous thunder of the guns on the battlefield of the Somme River.

During the week that followed the departure of the Scottish soldiers, we all experienced nervous tension in the trenches, because for the first time we alone were directly and unsupported facing the enemy. We always expected an attack, and were always ready to hasten our defensive positions, because we had not yet learned all the aspects of the trench life. However, we soon learned what to do and fortunately for us, our adversaries were generally inactive. In addition to the usual daily firing, grenade throwing and the night shooting up of flares, nothing noteworthy happened. With us it really was 'in the West is nothing new'.

On 26 July I and my friend Winkle Webster were pleased to be ordered to leave the front in order to go to Le Touquet for an instruction course on the Lewis machine-gun. So, we quickly obeyed the order and went back to Maroeuil. The next day, we walked up to Bray and we boarded a train to go to via Aubigny to Étaples, from where we walked the camp at Le Touquet.

Le Touquet, in ordinary times, is a well known French seaside resort and there they had set up a firing range and a school where they could improve the knowledge and use of machine guns. The surroundings were beautiful, by the sea, and the weather was beautiful, and we both enjoyed a beautiful holiday.

Here are the notes from my diary: -

July 30. Awoke 6.30;   paraded 9.30 for instruction; Midday meal 12.00; a swim in the sea with my friend Webster – tea 16.30
July 31. Awoke 5.30m; paraded for gymnastics 7.00; breakfast 8.00;   paraded for instruction 9.00; midday meal 13.00;   paraded for instruction 14.15; after tea went with Webster to Paris Plage' spent an interesting and amusing evening exploring the town.
August 1. parades similar to yesterday – then an evening lecture by Russell Lovell on "The War."

August 2. parades as before; an afternoon swim;
concert in the evening.
That day we were examined about our knowledge of the use of the machine-gun, and I successfully passed this exam and was now able to instruct on it. I then received additional pay for this skill.

August 3. woke up at 6.30; breakfast at 7.00, then swam in the sea; midday meal at 1pm; tea at 3.30pm.

Then we left the camp and walked to the station railway at Étaples; here we boarded a train and travelled to Abbeville, where we arrived at 11.30 at night. We found some kind of place to sleep near to the station, but didn't get much sleep, as we were told that we should soon be resuming the journey. Finally we got on a train in the early morning and on August 4, at 6.30 our train left Abbeville; the train was a slow one and at 10.30 we reached St. Pol and finally at midday we arrived in Aubigny. From there we walked to the headquarters of our division in Hermaville. Here we had a sleep in a tent. On August 5, we left Hermaville and walked to Bray. During the afternoon we rested and in the evening we left Bray. It so happened that the day after Webster and I left the trenches, our regiment withdrew to Bray for a rest and clean-up, but they went back on the 4th August. So Webster and I travelled with the regimental postman in a truck to the reserve line at Neuville St. Vaast, which was close to the Sapper dugout. Here we saw the arrival by night of the food etc. for the regiment in the line. The trucks brought all sorts of supplies to this place and soldiers waited in line to unload all the various things and put them in piles along the road. An officer supervised this. The regimental sergeant-major showed a paper to the officer, which was signed. The regimental sergeant-major then shows the paper to the sergeant-major of the portering party, and he sends his men to pick up the necessary things. So much tea, so much sugar, quantities of oatmeal, of jam, of cheese, of small tins of meat, sometimes butter, also some fresh meat or of bacon, very many biscuits, and sometimes bread. In addition to the foodstuffs there were military stores - cartridges, pumps, wood and iron to build or repair the dugouts, barbed wire etc.

21

With the regimental sergeant-major was a party of porters, who put the various goods, bags, etc on their backs to carry them forward. All this was done as quickly and quietly as possible, for the enemy was not very far away, and from time to time they heard sounds and immediately fired salvos of shells at us. This place was always particularly dangerous at night, as the Germans probably knew about the nightly delivery of these necessities, as they occasionally shelled us. However the porters did not come at the same time each night and they left as soon as possible. Leaving Sappers Dugout, they soon reached the place where the regimental cooks worked, and there gave them the cooking items. There was also a share out of other things in groups, one group for each company, according to the number of soldiers in the company. People from each company waited here for the arrival of the other porters, and after the share out the company porters took these goods, which were appropriate to their own company. It was with these porters, that Webster and I went forward to the first line in Doublement trench. There we met a member from every section of the company and who, after a further share out, took the food for the next day to his comrades. The captain told Webster and me to find our comrades, and so we parted because he had to go down to one of the positions that were at the end of a narrow trench in front of the first line. I had to go to a small dugout on the right flank of the line. So, early in the morning, I went via concealed ways to find my comrades.

Finally I reached the place I sought, and saw the sentry in the No. 3 machine gun position at the end of Douai trench. Almost immediately I heard the voice of his companion who said, "Halt, who is coming?" and although I could not see the speaker, I recognized the voice of a comrade and spoke to make sure that I was identified as a friend. I went forward and soon saw him in a corner where he stood with a hand grenade ready to defend the position and raise the alarm if some enemy had penetrated so far into defense system. We greeted each other sincerely and chatted a bit about the events of the period when I was away, but I was very tired and very anxious to sleep.

The person who had recently changed the guard and the sentry then went into the dugout to sleep. So I went after them, but before I could go down, I had to rearrange my equipment and take off my back the bag in which were all my belongings, especially, coat, etc. I started to do that, and just sorted out a few things when I heard the sound of a shell in the air. Instinctively I started to throw myself into the entrance of the dugout, and at the same time there was a loud noise near to me. I received a strong push in the back, and fell down the six steps into the dugout. The candle, which burned my friend as he went in, immediately went out. I found myself among my comrades, a little shaken but otherwise not damaged. They woke up and I quickly shouted that it was just me, so that they would not think that I am an enemy and shoot me. Then we all laughed at my sudden and undignified return to the group and then we examined the dugout to find out if there was any damage. We found that the shell had hit the beam over the entrance of the dugout and of course, if I had not heard it coming and thrown myself down, I would have been also harmed. As it happened, there was a piece of the shell in my bag, which had gone through an iron plate, and lay in the middle of a box of cigarettes, which I brought back to give to friends. This was the cause of the punch that pushed me down the stairway. So, it seems that this return was almost the end of my military service, and we were all delighted by my lucky escape. The things that I put down at the entrance were widely scattered, particularly my haversack, which contained my food, I never saw again; my rifle was at the end of the trench, and I found my cup out in the trench later in the day. So, the next day I had to get some new things.

We stayed in the No. 3 position till the 12th of August and then another regiment came to replace us, and we went back to the third line next to Sappers shelter. In this line, we could rest a little more because it was not necessary to have the sentry duties that were necessary in the first line. But there was one unpleasant activity , and that was when the goods needed by the regiment arrived by horse-carts from the town of Maroeuil. I've described this, as all of us hated this task because of the frequent shelling of the place. So during our time here, it was decided to slightly to increase the quanties of necessities in the hidden stores by the wayside a little away from the place where we then lived. So, at night we sweated as we worked to unload the various things and put them in the store. At the same time we heartily cursed the Germans, who shelled the place and also the officer who organised the delivery of provisions. On the third night, two of our company were injured while working here; but of course, the work continued just the same.

On the 16th of August we again moved up to the first line, but not at the same position. This time we went to No. 1 position, at the end of Rawson Street. One evening, on the 20th of August, when I went to the place where I had to stand to watch the enemy trench, a piece of shrapnel from a shell, that exploded in the air somewhere near by, hit my arm. In fact it was only a small piece, which only pierced the skin and stayed fixed there. I extracted it, and, because it was so small I didn't give it much thought, and so I went in and replaced my comrade in the duty room. I told him the episode and then he left. I and my partner stayed on duty and soon an officer came, who asked "where is the wounded man?". I explained that only a small piece struck me, and that did not seem to affect me. However, he said that I must not stay there, but should to go to the doctor so that he could bandage the wound. So, I had to collect my belongings and made the long walk back to the third line, where the regimental doctor was located. Because I expected to go back immediately after the wound was bandaged, I was somewhat annoyed with the officer because of his order. Then imagine my surprise when the doctor ordered me to go to the hospital in Hautevesne for an inoculation! It seemed that everyone who is injured, even the most unimportant, has to be inoculated against tetanus, which in this region was the cause of a lot of deaths. So, they put me on a stretcher in a Red Cross vehicle, and above me on another stretcher, laid the body of a man from a regiment who died of a bullet through the head. We travelled at night, the two of us as strange companions, and every time the vehicle bounced, due to shell holes by the road, I was afraid that my fellow traveller would fall on me. I was very glad when they stopped near the cemetery and took him out of the vehicle. In the hospital, they gave me a place to sleep in a bed. What a luxury! It was a real bed with blankets and pillow; for the first time in three months. I didn't argue, so I just went to bed and after smoking a cigarette, feeling like a millionaire, I slept deeply. In the morning, they woke me up to give me food and then I got up, had the inoculation and the arm re-bandaged. Of course, because it was so small, and I was young and strong, it soon healed, but I stayed there, for three days, as if in paradise. Then in the evening, of the 23 of August, I went back by the now well-known way via Bray to Sappers shelter and then to our position in the first line. On 24 August, in the evening, we received information that a group of 20 men from our regiment intended to attack the German lines to bomb a dugout and, if possible, to take some prisoners. Consequently we all had to stay alert. It was a very dark evening and night. The guns of the two opposing armies were almost silent. However the Germans in trenches opposite us seemed to be a bit nervous, as they put up more flares more frequently than usual. We did not do the same, however more and more flares illuminated the darkness. Just before midnight, one could almost feel the unusual silence. Suddenly, without warning, our artillery and machine guns opened up, and for twenty minutes they rained iron on the site, to be attacked; after the firing aimed specifically at the place had stopped, and our attackers advanced to do their work. Of course, the Germans immediately and wholeheartedly returned the fire and the silent night became like hell. The assault party returned, carrying one dead, some wounded and brought in a dozen prisoners. Gradually the thunder decreased until it was not much more than the usual barrage. Presently another regiment came to replace us and we returned to the village of Bray. We arrived there at 7.15 in the morning, after an exciting night, feeling very tired. My company was sited in a hut near a stream; in the hut we found a collection of beds made of wire mesh and a small amount of food, then we all slept. Next day they woke us and again we ate, and began to clean ourselves. Then they paid us some money and we went to Maroeuil and spent a happy evening in the pubs eating well cooked omelettes, drinking and singing until it was time for us to go back for sleep. It was just as well that some of us were not drunk.

We stayed and rested for seven days in the town of Bray. How quickly these days passed in the much more peaceful atmosphere away from the front! As usual the "rest" involved a lot of work - but the important point was that one could take clothes off at night to sleep and could move around without the fear of being the target of a bullet or a shell. Yes, far too quickly our stay in Bray came to an end and at a cold time on the 1st of September, we replaced the 15th Regiment in Paris Redoubt.

My machine gun section went to a dugout in the Paris Redoubt, a place where we hadn't done duty before. Because it was in the main line, we had more protection than the sites in the most forward trenches. There was shelter both against the weather, the sun and the enemy's deadly fire. Here in the first line the dugouts were really deep underground, where everyone could sleep in the dry and warm. Apart from that, there was more activity around the headquarters of the company, and we saw a lot of things that were happening. In our former place of duty, it was too dangerous to move during daylight and because of that we were almost isolated there. Apart from that, it was much more dangerous here, because we were close enough to the enemy line and sometimes one of their night patrols came near us in the dark by mistake. Furthermore, sometimes we were subjected to not only enemy shells, but also badly aimed shells from our own guns. So, when they had sent us to the comparatively good position in Paris Redoubt, we were very glad.

The 6th of September was an exciting night. Early in the morning, the 7th, the Germans detonated a mine in the proximity of the machine gun position in Claudot Sap. At the moment when the explosion occurred, I was in the dugout, at our place in Paris Redoubt, and there one experienced a big shock. The walls seemed to be moving forward and back. Earth fell from the ceiling. We all hurried out, ready for anything. Outside bombardment raged. But no one was moving in front of us. But we thought that perhaps some kind of attack would be coming. So, ears and eyes were strained to catch signs of movements by the enemy, we stood there prepared. I was on

26

one side of the position, grenade in hand ready to throw it immediately if the enemy should appear in the trench. All of a sudden I received a blow on the head. I almost jumped out of my skin, assuming that an unseen enemy got at me from outside of the trench. However, I saw that the assailant was not human, but a piece of wood, which an exploding shell had thrown into the air from near the trench. The piece of wood had fallen across the trench; my head was a little above the level of the ground; and, because of that, unfortunately the piece was able to hit me. Later, someone else replaced me in that position, and I went to help our corporal with the gun. Pretty soon we realized that just to the right of us there was hand-to-hand fighting in the English trenches. Gradually the enemy retreated without success and we then fired our gun at them. Later we were told that the explosion had made a huge crater, and we were on one side and the Germans on the other. Our regiment lost several comrades, but it is thought that the attackers lost many more.

On the night of the 7th of September we left Paris Redoubt to go to the second line, where we remained in reserve. We stayed there until the 13th of September, when we returned to hold the no.1 machine gun position in Rawson Street. We stayed there for six days. After the excitement of the attack, we have now found a peaceful enough life. On the 19th we left and again walked back down the long trench way and finally we reached the town of Bray to enjoy an extra rest period.

During my life as a soldier during the war, I was happy about one thing. That was that I have never experienced a gas attack. I had never to use my anti-gas mask to protect me from the evil intentions of my adversaries. However, I did use the mask in gas. This happened during my rest period in Bray, on 23th September 1916. In order to check the effectiveness of our gas protection, we all went through a room full of poison gas. I did not notice anything unusual for my mask was quite good. At first we became used to carrying them, because we had often exercised and walked for hours, carrying the anti-gas equipment. However we have always cursed the uncomfortable things!!

When we returned to the trenches, on 25 September, we will soon notice a difference. The enemy will become more and more active with artillery and mortars. They had a trench mortar, that threw a bomb, which weighed a hundred pounds. Against life it was not very effective, because the bombs came slowly and we could see them and flee to safer place. But, where it fell, these bombs always made a great noise and damage. Not only that, but the range for our trench seemed to be well known and they have done a lot to us. Every night it was active and heavily damaged our trenches so that we had to work hard to restore them. As a result we were very tired. We could not sleep more than rather five to six hours in total in a day; and this we could not get continuously, but only from time to time.

On 30 September we again did a night attack against the enemy to capture their soldiers to gain information. Perhaps our side suspected that the additional activity was a sign of a big attack. The thing went well, very similar to that of the 24th of August, but we lost a few more men. So as usual, after such attack, we went back to serve in the second line. But there was no more rest. Due to the frequent repair and restoration of the trenches we had to bring forward a lot of material for that work. Finally, our section had to take another turn in the first line. The regiment there increasingly suspected attack and asked for night support. So, we went forward and climbed out of the trench to cross the ground to some hole where we had to stay the whole night. From time to time we saw passing hostile groups but we were not allowed to shoot. They did not want to reveal our positions until the expected attack. So, we would not shoot until they sent into the air a green signal, which would show the beginning of the attack; or on the other hand, if a party should come straight at us. This duty lasted three nights for us. Later, it was thought that the attack would not occur and we did not return to those positions after the 4th of October.

On the 7th we left our rest place in the second line and went to the place in Claudot Sap, near the place where the great explosion had occurred. But the Germans seem to be no longer interested in the place because there we spent a comparatively peaceful week until 13 October, when we went back to Bray for the longed for real rest. So we slept there! Again this time we did a lot of parade ground exercises. Because we had done real fighting, we had not often done these, but during this time, we had to do those tedious ceremonials. The Reason! Well, on the 18th there was a big parade and a number of generals and other eminents came to inspect us. They presented medals to one officer and two soldiers, who acted very bravely during the attack on 30th of September.

On the 19th we again made our nightly walk back into the line, early in the morning on the 20th my section was again on duty in the lookout post in Forges Gap (No. 6 Post). That day my friend Johnnie Bullock was on duty during the morning and looked out with the periscope while we took a nap. After a time he woke us. We cursed him and asked him about the reason. Hear! He said. We listened. Nothing happened. Nothing was heard. Well! What? He replied that he was hearing sounds tap, tap, tap, as if someone was digging under the ground. Neither we, nor he could hear anything and we made fun of him and said that he dreamed or was trigger happy. Finally, one after another we went back to sleep. We heard nothing more during the day and we all decided that Johnnie in fact imagined the matter. But, in the evening, while we drank tea, which was sent forth to us from the first line, Johnnie said again suddenly, "Hear, that's the sound again." We all laughed at him, but he insisted that we listened carefully. And one by one we all heard a tap, tap, tap - pause - tap, tap, tap - pause - tap, tap, tap. This went on. After a long pause. Again the sounds. We all looked at each other. Certainly, it was possible someone was digging beneath us. It was then about the time when we expect the arrival of the officer who occasionally visits all the groups to receive the reports and news from the soldiers of all that was happening. So, in the meantime we decided to wait for his arrival and report to him. But, in the meantime, we have almost ceased to chat to better hear the sounds. We did not feel very happy, because in this region a there was a lot of tunneling and we had made large explosions under the enemy. When it was dark, the officer came. But a little before then those underground stopped digging, and of course neither we nor him could hear anything. However, nothing happened and he went. From time to time during the night, we heard the digging. When another officer came in the morning, he also heard the sound, and reported the matter to the captain. Then they sent an officer of an engineers regiment to listen. Nothing is heard. During the day there was quiet. At night, again the digging began. In the morning an engineer came up with instruments and stayed to listen. His diagnosis was that someone must be digging. However, they did not seem to be advancing, and because of this he assumed that they had made the place in which to place the explosive. As they were no longer digging, the engineer said that the enemy must have put in the explosive. Consequently one might expect the explosion at some time after the cessation of the sounds. The sounds had ceased. The engineer left to report. He predicted an exciting night. Presently an officer came and ordered that immediately after dusk we should leave that location to start building another position on the same trench but a little closer to our front line. How long the hours seemed until sunset. We became more and more nervous, at the thought of the invisible death under our feet. With relief, we finally received the order to leave that place. The moon rose and it was a beautiful night. But that did not matter to us. Our only goal was to dig ourselves a new firing position for our machine-gun and a shelter from the flying pieces of iron from our adversaries. The place we chose, was on right hand side of the trench, which went forward to our recently abandoned position. On the left, on the other side of the forward going trench, the bomber section were to built us a new observation post. We bet them that we would complete our position before they came. Higher and higher the moon rose, and deeper and deeper we dug. Behind us many of the soldiers stood ready for the warning from the engineers. From time to time they brought in more ammunition for us and more bombs for the bombers. The officers were waiting for an attack after the next explosion. The trenches in our neighbourhood were silent and peaceful. Only occasionally there was the bright light of the flares that the Germans had shot into the air. We also used flares, but those of the Germans were much more effective. In the distance we could see and hear the signs of fighting. It has always been like this on a night before a major incident. Suddenly, it was as if there was an earthquake. The whole earth around us shuddered. After that a loud noise. Then the air was full of material. Large pieces dropped everywhere. We could not see anything. Almost simultaneously there was the crackle of rifles, machine guns and the thunder of the artillery. The air was filled with earth and iron. Shrill sounds. Explosions everywhere around. I was very amazed that none of us was wounded. After a very short time our rifles, machine guns and artillery entered the fray. We were too close to the centre of the action. Much shrapnel from both sides fell like rain around us. I saw in the light of the explosions that rats were desperately rushing away. One huge rat tried to flee; but he has no hind quarters. All these things happen in a few minutes - even seconds. Then Johnnie noticed shapes to the right of us. They came out of the enemy trenches. Our machine gun began to speak. She spoke continuously. Chattered for a long time. But the enemy did not come towards us, but went to the right, where they attacked the nearby company of my regiment. At the same time, the bombers next to us saw that another attack had occurred against the left flank of our company and the neighbouring regiment. So, the Germans did not react in the same way as after the previous occasion, when they attacked directly at the place where the explosion occurred. Instead this time they advanced to both sides of the site of the explosion. Due to the fact that we had heard those sounds and warned the officer, the commander had been able sent more soldiers into the trenches. Consequently the enemy had met very strong resistance and after a few optimistic attempts to enter our trenches, they had to abandon the attempt. It became quiet. Someone noticed that the moon had already set. Also in the sky in front of us we could see the signs of daylight. Once again one had time to notice sensations returning and we realised that we were very cold. Then one of the bombers asked how we are doing. Among them were two injured and it was expected that stretcher bearers would take one of them back to the hospital. The other wounded man had been struck in the arm, and he walked away. The wounded man who remained looked pale and very ill, but we tried to comfort him and cheer him with the thought that he would soon be out of the war and possibly again in the beloved homeland. Meanwhile, the place became increasingly quiet. The morning came gray and cold and we rejoiced when they sent warm tea forward to us. So ended another 'surprise' and we resumed the daily routine again.

The next night a very horrible thing happened that extremely upset every one of us, and especially for everyone in our own company. One of the staff officers of the Brigade visited the battalion. He came alone without announcement and wandered from place to place and finally found one sentry who was asleep during the day. Of course this is a serious and unforgivable crime and the officer immediately arrested the culprit, who was sent for trial. We were very sad, firstly because of the shame that came to our regiment, but most of all because the fate of our comrade. In fact, he was very young soldier, not much more than a boy, who had recently arrived from England. He, like all of us, was completely exhausted from lack of sleep, long work and exciting nights. We all knew that such sleepiness could easily happen with any of us. Our nerves were taut because of the dangerous situation, and in which we had all to be always ready to repel an enemy attack. At the same time we lacked sufficient sleep and finally nature becomes more and more demanding, up to the point when you have to sleep, just sleep, whether you are in danger or not. I remembered something like that happened to me once, sometime before. One night, as I stood on look-out during a storm, I thought I heard movement in front of me. I listened. Then I heard a sound. Again silence. To be able to listen more attentively, I supported my head on my hands, and looked forward with every ability. I do not know what happened after that until I woke up, feeling something on my hand next to my face. My first glance showed me a big rat, who ran away down the other arm. Uh! I then knew that I had fallen asleep. What a dangerous situation! And I noted that this happened at a time when I felt in great danger. Suppose that wasn't a rat that had woken me, but staff officer!! Terrible thought!! Yes, we are all very sad and sympathized with our poor comrade, whom they walked away, probably to the death of shame at the hands of comrades. In fact, we received information that they sentenced him to death.

On 21 October a very exciting aerial combat took place over our sector. A group of aeroplanes, our's and their's, fought very low over us. Back and forth, now over our lines, then over the Germans, they flew in mortal combat. Always, when possible, we fired with rifles and machine guns against the enemy aeroplanes. Of course our firing was limited because of the danger of hitting one of our fliers. Finally, one of the Germans was damaged and landed just behind the enemy line. Soon after that, the combatants separated and flew home.

In fact, during this period the airmen were very aggressive and there were frequent aerial battles. Both sides were very agile and strong, and we saw a lot of spectacular aerial acrobatics. One day, we saw a remarkable thing. A series of German aeroplanes flew over our trenches. Presently they were confronted by a group of English aeroplanes. But before the two sides met together in battle, our anti-aircraft guns shot against the advancing Germans. One shrapnel shell exploded directly under one of the aeroplanes, which immediately turned and quickly fell to the ground, turning back and forth as it went. It fell towards our lines, and we looked at it wondering whether or not the aviator would die in the descent. Suddenly, when the aeroplane had almost reached the ground, the aviator restarted the engine, the aeroplane recovered its balance and flew away to the German side. We all marvelled at the courage and admired the skill of the German aviator.

On 22 October a strange thing happened to me. It seems that due to the frequent destruction of our trenches by the enemies heavy trench mortars, our commanders decided to retaliate and at the same time try to destroy some enemy trench mortars. In the middle of the day we received the order to leave our advanced position because of the danger from our mortar bombs aimed at nearby German positions. So, we carefully obeyed and went to an underground shelter in the main line, to wait until the end of the action. Going ahead as planned, a little after three in the afternoon, our mortars began a barrage of the enemy position. Around four o'clock some people came with our tea. In the morning, we had received postal packages from home, and we all had cakes or other dainties. So, we decided to set up a party here in the dugout. So that's what we did and began to enjoy a delicious tea. Meanwhile, our 'friends', the enemy, disdained our 'donated' mortar bombs, and sent us a lot of their own. So, while we celebrated in the dugout, over our heads there was a furious barrage. Suddenly a heavy bomb fell on the ground just above our heads and exploded with great noise. This caused a lot of earth to fall from our roof to the ground. Each of us was buried up to the waist. None were injured, or suffered any sort of injury. Our steel hats had protected our heads. Our "tasty tea" had completely disappeared. Then when we realized what had happened, we all burst out laughing. But none of us could move because the weight of the earth around the lower part of our bodies prevented any movement. Comrades from another dugout noticed that the bomb hit our shelter and one of them ran to see whether or not we were alive. He fetched two or three others and we were soon released. But our nice tea was completely wasted and we lost a lot of other things under the earth. It was fortunate for us that the ground, in which the shelter was dug, was soft.

During these days rumours spread about a wholescale movement of the whole division. We speculated about the possiblity of a long rest somewhere away from the battle line and then intense preparations to take part in some sort of attack in the region of the River Somme. More and more the rumours came, until at last it was known that we had to go to another part of the line after a break.

A Canadian regiment came on the 25th of October, the 52A Canadian Battalion, and we left our sector. So, for the last time we went back along those long trenches and reached Maroeuil at 7.30 in the evening. They paid us some money and we immediately rushed to the bar to eat and drink, and forget the dangers that we have just left behind.

Oh, what a beautiful evening! Such evenings of drink and song and abandon were very sweet and propitiatory to life after a period of strain in the war zone. In Maroeuil we slept that night in unoccupied houses, a little damaged due to former barrage, but good enough perches.

During the following days we walked. To us these days were enjoyable, because we were away from explosions and the narrow life of the trenches. The trees and fields looked normal. In the fields there grew green herbs, vegetables, flowers, and not stakes, barbed wire, human bones, etc. And the air is fresh and clean. Yes, while we were walking, we quickly regained our cheerfulness and good humour. The journey was quite normal, with little interest. At night we slept in barns, which were much more comfortable than the trench corner or underground shelter.

On the 26th we reached Hermanville, 27th Mons-en-Ternios, 28th Fortel and 29th Montingny Jongleurs. Here we remained until the 3rd of November, and carried out a number of military exercises.

The 3rd of November was the anniversary of my day of birth, and so I had reached my nineteenth year; that is, that I have reached the age at which one would normally enlist as a soldier; and now I had been a soldier for 21 months. That day we walked to Buigny L'Abbe and my section was living in a farm, which belonged to the mayor. We stayed there until the 15th, and I became friends with a young boy named Victoire, with whom I had become able to test my ability to speak French. The conversations were very simple, but I progressed. This was the first and only time that I could enjoy using the French language. On Sunday, 5th, we were at Disernon. On Monday, 6th, our company walked to Abbeville for a bath, after which they allowed us to wander about until the evening. There I spent an interesting time with some friends. One of the things I noticed most was the cathedral in Abbeville. It stands next to a square and in the to the memory after so many years (now 1933). One thing that I better remember is that I went to the barber and he cut my hair. After I left the barbers shop, I remembered that I had not washed my head for a long time, and presumably it was very dirty. I blush with shame when I think about what the barber would think of me. In Abbeville, I experimented with liqueurs for the first time. They were sweet and warm, but not very cheering. But, when next morning I was suffering from a terrible headache, then I swore an oath to myself that I would never drink liqueurs again.

We stayed in Buigny L'Abbé until the 15th of November. The period was our first normal military "rest". This consisted of unnecessary work and parades. But every day more strange rumours came. We will not go to the Somme battlefield, but perhaps to India, China, Egypt, Russia, in fact anywhere there was war or British soldiers. Some favoured people received special leave to go to England. Day followed day and the rumours became more and more varied.

On the 15th, however, we began to wonder. First of all we walked to Longpré, which we reached in the evening. On the 9th we entrained in normal wagons (for eight horses or forty people) and we went on our way to somewhere - we did not know where. We finally left Longpré on the 10th, in the evening and we proceded in a way typical of that to which we had become accustomed in France during the war. Long delays. Fast forward movement. All the time there were great bumps, big jerks and the noise of our cattle trucks. You will understand something of the rate and type of journey, if I recount the names of cities through which we went. After an exciting night, with this start-stop travelling, by the middle of the day of the 16th of ovember, we got to Versailles (Seine-et-Oise). When we went through Amiens we had to pass by a train, which stood in the station with two wagons fiercely burning. This was a hot experience, and our wagons were filled with smoke. However, no wagon of our train caught on fire and we safely left Amien on the way to Versailles; once through that place and district we went faster. Then we stopped for some time in Montereau (Seine en Marne) to eat.

During the night we continue to journey, and finally in the morning of the 17th we reached Macon, and stopped for breakfast. That morning we passed through the great station of Lyons, where we saw other trains full of French soldiers. Very brave looking young French soldiers in their blue-gray uniforms. After Valence, in the evening we stopped again in Pierrelatte (Drôme) where we ate and found enough water for good bathe. After a long enough stop, during which we could pleasantly "stretch our legs", we continued on our way through the night.

Finally we reached the southern coastal port of Marseilles on 18th of November just when the first lights of the new day appeared in the sky. We were then very cold, with the usual chill of the early morning. Also the reputedly famous blue sky was covered with grey rain-bearing clouds that sped across the sky, driven by a cold wind. We walked to the camp, which was located on the side of a hill that overlooks the bay. The wind soon blew away the clouds, and the blue sky reappeared and the warm sun shone upon us, pleasing us. The camp consisted of a set of white tents, set among the trees on the hill. The sight of the tents was delightfully beautiful, and we could see an island in the bay a little way from the shore. When the sun shone on this view, it was really worth seeing. We stayed there until the 22th of the month. We did not do a lot. Only a little instruction about our machine gun. They did not allow us to go into the city without special permission. I received such permission one afternoon and with some friends wandered through town. Everything appeared to be novel and worth seeing. But there was not much time. The large number of different nationalities, clothing, faces, etc. especially interested me. My impression of that visit is now very confusing. When we returned to the camp that night they commanded us to report to the tent of the doctor so that we could be inoculated against venereal disease. Because this presupposed a relationship with a prostitute, and because none of my friends even thought of that, and because we never intended to do that, we all refused to obey the order. We were all very indignant. They threatened punishment and made a list of the names of those disobeying. I do not know why, but no one received any punishment for this disobedience, which would normally result in very severe punishment. The weather was kind and our stay near Marseilles was one of the most enjoyable episodes in my military wanderings.

On the 22nd we packed our belongings in our backpacks and walked to the pier where we embarked on the steamship "Megantic," one of the great "White Star" ships, which in the beautiful days of peace travelled across the

Atlantic Ocean between the United States and England. It was famous for one thing. It was the ship, on which once a man called Crippen was brought back, he had murdered his wife in London and had escaped to the United States along with his stenographer. The murder, escape, hunt, capture and trial of the man made a great sensation in the city at that time.

When we went on board we were very surprised. The interior of the boat was just the same as during its normal peacetime journeys. I and three comrades occupied a cabin in which there were four bunks - real beds with mattresses, pillows, sheets and blankets - two bunks on top, two bunks below. We are very happy with this because soldiers do not usually travel in so much luxury. Later in the day, they called us to the dining room and there were polished tables, armchairs, a carpet on the floor. After our months in the trenches the whole thing seemed to us either a mistake or a dream. But it was true, we sat in the armchairs next to the polished tables, on which we put our crude military cups, cutlery and plates. To me this seemed criminal. But then the dream ended. The food was the usual hard biscuits, large tins of jam, rancid butter and some kind of drink. We were told that it was tea, but I've never tasted anything like it. Later I came across such a flavour on other troopships. My opinion was that the water was heated in a big pot; this was never emptied of water, but more was added for the next mealtime, along with either some tea, coffee or cocoa; because the resulting beverage was a mixture with an indistinguishable taste.

After dinner we explored the ship and found more luxuries, among them the best were the baths with hot water - salt or fresh. And we said to ourselves - 'Look, this is a good war, right? After the usual work, duties and orders, we very soon went to bed, firstly because we are tired, but secondly to enjoy our newly found luxury. I was soon asleep.

Sometime early in the morning I woke up. I soon realised that the ship was moving strongly and rolling in all directions. The voyage had begun while we slept. The other occupants of the cabin left their bunks one by one. So, I got up and dressed myself and went up to the deck. It was certainly a very early hour because in the sky there was a half-moon. Passing the lavatory, I looked, and there I saw the reason for my friends' empty bunks. The place was full of sick people, the most of whom suffered so much that their only wish was to die. Oh, the cruelty of the sea goddesses! Oh, weakness of human pride and glory! These brave soldiers of a proud empire - look at them after so short an experience of the sea waves. But I had to hurry away; the disgusting sight almost made me another victim. So, as soon as possible I got up into the cool, fresh, salt air of a new morning. In the sky were masses of clouds that moved so fast that one might assume that they fled from a terrible, angry god. Around the boat there was a raging storm. The waves were grey and troubled. Like tortured animals they jumped towards the sky, only to later fall back wearily. And as they could not punish the wind that so troubled them, they threw themselves against our ship as if to sink it as a peace offering to reconcile the angry wind god. And our boat, although it was large, feeling the strong blows of the waves against her, stumbled here and there, with a very distressing effect on those who were ill. I felt well myself. I had often been asked whether or not I would be a good sailor. And, here's the answer. On quite a rough sea I did not feel ill, but cheerful and well. So I wandered around the decks. From one side I saw a boat. It was a naval vessel. One of our accompanying escorts. Then I saw the other. But soon they both disappeared. Then, out of a cloud of sea spray one reappeared, and then another. So they travelled with us, and they probably went through the waves more often than over them. I thought of the sick below. How would they manage on that kind of boat. Behind us, I noticed a second transport ship, and on the other side two more escort vessels. The number of the nearest ship was T.B.D.02. Later, the other left us and we went ahead with T.B.D.02 alone.

I did not know why, maybe the officers were also sick, but we did not have a parade on the first day of the trip. The first time one heard reveille on the regimental bugle was to announce breakfast. For those who had fallen ill, when they heard this sound they just sighed heavily and felt worse. We, who were not ill and had a good appetite, hastened to the dining hall. One person from each table went to the kitchen to fetch the food. When they returned, we saw that the breakfast consisted mainly of mutton stew in which fairly large pieces of fat were floating. Quite a large number of those present left, other braver men remained for as long as they could, but finally had to give up. The remainder had a great meal, behaving as soldiers, as the situation required. After breakfast I went out on the deck to the rear part of the ship where I stood a long time watching the big waves, through which we sailed. One moment we are high in the air, the next down in the trough between two waves, where it seemed that the ship must be submerged.

After some time the order came that the machine guns should be located on the highest deck to watch for possible enemy submarines. Reportedly there were quite a large number of these boats, which were trying to sink transport ships. We were told that our task was to shoot, aiming at the turret of the submarine - not to damage it, as our bullets would not do that, but to as far as possible break up the surface of the water, around the turret, to obscure the vision of the attacker. I imagine that our small bullets, would not even do that very well. However, the situation didn't arise - as I will describe later.

But for us this was a very good duty and a very pleasant business. Firstly we did not have to do other more unpleasant duties and secondly on the upper deck we were alone and found plenty of space to lie comfortably and peaceably in the beautiful fresh sea air.

On 24 November we saw the island, Sardinia. But now the weather became fairer and we spent a pleasant time on the upper deck. While we are not on duty, we lay there reading, writing or even idly watching the sea, or even more lazily sleeping.

On the morning of the 26th we passed the island Malta, where the escort T.B.D.02 left us, another ship – T.B.D.69 joined us instead.

There was some excitement on the morning of the 28th. Suddenly there came a sound of a fog horn from another transport ship, that was traveling with us. It was an alarm signal to warn us that a submarine had been spotted. Whereupon our ship started fast but steady evasive movements. All the soldiers put on life jackets and took their allotted places near the lifeboats so that they could if necessary launch them should our ship be hit. We weren't to remain there with my section, and an officer sent us to another upper deck with the gun, where there was also the ship's gun. There we looked for a place to set up our gun for use if it was required.

While we did this the sailors, whose duty was firing this larger gun, noticed us. They had been too busy on their own duties. But then they asked "Hey! What are you doing here? ". We explained. They said "Well, you take your 'pea-shooter' away, because it is of no use here." We couldn't argue and had to leave, somewhat angered by the of the contempt of sailors for our machine gun.

Meanwhile, we heard firing from the escorts, but could not see anything. Later, the escort went somewhere to one side, and fired from time to time. But apparently they did not manage to hit our attacker. A little later we left our dangerous situation and resumed the usual daily shipboard way of life.

Chapter III

Salonika

In the summer of 1916 there was an ambitious proposal to make a huge push in the Balkan countries. The remainder of the Serbian army was ill equipped and ill disciplined; Romania was allied to the anti-German Nations; and it had been calculated that Bulgaria will be defeated and their fellow nations driven across the River Danube. The Romanian army, after some brief success, hopelessly fell apart because of the skillful strategy of General Mackensen. The army of the assailants again became defenders of the district around Salonika. Then followed a period when there was serious doubt about the safety of this army. It was thought that the victorious army might try to drive their opponents into the sea by the capture of the important port of Salonika, which could be an invaluable base for submarines in the eastern part of the Mediterranean.

More reinforcing corps were required, and indeed it was because of this our division, the 60th Division, so suddenly travelled away to the east from France.

Around this time, the relationship between the anti-German nations and King Constantine of Greece became very unfriendly. That ruler was known to be very pro-german and it was feared that if he succeeded in drawing his nation into the war on the side of the "Central Powers", this would probably occur at the same time as the attacks against Salonika by the Bulgarians from the north and the Greeks from the south. If this did happen, the army of the "anti-Germans" would be in a dangerous situation. The Greeks would have only two possible ways to advance. Both came through Larissa where, reportedly, most of the Greek army were gathering. One way would be along the shore of the Gulf of Salonika, east of Olympus. The other way would be through the steep pass of Petra.

General Sarrail, commander-in-chief of the "Anti-Germans" army decided to block both ways by the occupation of the city Katerini, where the two roads meet to the north of the mountain; and where, by the establishment of defensive positions in tactical locations, he could block the progress of the Greeks on the lower plains. The railway, which links Salonika and the Southern Greece had for a long time been badly maintained, and in many places it was completely damaged by the recent heavy rains.

It was decided, therefore, that our Brigade should go by boat on the sea to Uromeri, a village six miles from Katerini to act as the vanguard of the expedition. Meanwhile the animal transport and the artillery would march by road from Salonika to Katerini.

This, then, was the situation when we arrived in the port of Salonika after the delightful shipboard journey. From the place where our ship was in dock, we could see a street. This was a place of interest because of the Greek letters above the shops and for the different aspect of the faces of the passers-by, also the clothes that seemed a little unusual to us. But we did not find much time to look at or think about such things. Here we are on land. Once on land we had work to do. So we needed to land as quickly as possible. These kinds of movements of the regiment give rise to a lot of work, and as usual we soldiers worked perspiring. Finally, everything and everyone were in Salonika. Soon the order came to put on our backpacks and to forward march through the city.

The strongest impression that I got from the city was of the dirt, but perhaps that was because we were walking through the dock district. In all countries the dockland districts of the cities are always a bit unpleasant. We have seen many different types of uniform among the soldiers, which we passed. Presumably these were the members of almost every nation, who were fighting against the Germans. But our backpacks were heavy and as we had not carried them during the recent two weeks, they felt even heavier than usual. So, we stopped looking at the city as we walked, and more closely looked at the road, that was in bad condition, and had holes in it which caused the unwary to fall. Finally, we left the city and went a little over nine kilometres to a point where a camp was found between some hills. This place was called Dudular Camp and located in a nice enough place. Indeed we were glad to reach it, first because we highly disliked our backpacks, and secondly because it was said that there was a cup of tea awaiting us. In addition, the weather was beautiful and we thought that this place much better than the trenches in France. We then did not know what we would doing next, but why think about that; here is a good place, nice weather, plenty of food, and during the first day nothing to do, so enjoy it.

But on the first of December the situation changed somewhat. Firstly, we went to a place away from the camp, where we found a huge bunch of mules. There was frequent hoof kicking in the lines. It is said that they were untrained mules, who had recently come directly from South America. Each of us got two of them, along with a piece of rope with which we led them. Imagine me! Young person born in a big city who does not even know anything about horses, let alone mules, and who suddenly finds himself the owner of two ill tempered unfriendly mules. My heart was in my mouth. However, I firmly held my rope and prayed for a good journey. Although many mules managed to escape and gallop away on the plain, hunted by desperate and cursing London-Scots, I happily reached the camp without accident, though once or twice I almost became a mule hunter. In the camp we tied our pets to long iron chains fastened between two bars and left them there. We were then given two nosebags, one for each mule. Also we received hay and grain to put into the nosebags. Then we had to take the animals to the near-by river to water them. When we got back, the first meal for the mules took place. What a situation! All the mules ran wild when they smelled the food. Hooves flew in every direction. Many of us received hoof kicks. It was a very difficult thing to fix a nosebag on the head of a mule that had become half wild from hunger, and that at the same time it is afraid of the nosebag, especially when the second mule of the pair becomes excited because it does not have a nosebag and hoof attacks everything next to it. But finally I had fastened the two bags on the heads of my mules and managed to get out safely.

44

Then we received, in a sack, a large number of pieces of leather, iron, and so on. Here was the harness for your mules, which had to be assembled. I did not know what to do first, so I waited until one of the regular carriers showed me these things.

Now I'd given much thought to the situation and told myself that if I want to have a peaceful life, somehow I had to get myself a pair of friendly mules. The present pair were too stubborn and too militant. I told myself that undoubtedly the professional carrier from his expert knowledge had chosen good friendly animals. So, the way to provide myself with a good pair would be a stealthy exchange of my beasts with those of one of the carriers. So I led my animals, one at a time, to the most distant group and there chose a mule on whose bridle is the name of the carrier, switched the reins and led the new animal away. The experiment was very well managed, and, although the owners of my new mules looked for the missing ones, they did not recognize them, and I had won a sweet pair.

The next day, a new comedy began. We had to harness up the yokes on the mules. The animals probably did not understand the idea. They either greatly feared the feel of the yoke, whose iron pieces made musical noise when we moved them, or they realized what this new devilry meant for them, more slavery and more work. But no matter, the fact is that they wholeheartedly rebelled against us in every possible way. And believe me, a rebellious mule is an undesirable animal. But by the old trick of a combined attack on each animal, one after the other, we finally harnessed up all yokes.

Later another even more amusing thing occurred (that is only amusing for the spectators), when we began to learn harnessing various types of packages. When you remember that you had to carry all the heavy items, that the regiment would need in their daily peaceful or military life, one can form some idea of the difficulties that the layout of such baggage on the mule presented to us, especially those of us who were inexperienced. But everything eventually ends, and behold, after a long struggle we humans had won, and each mule stood loaded, while we are weary sitting nearby, smoking a delicious cigarette. We left them to stand for a while so that they became accustomed to the loads. The colonel came and inspected the laden animals. Previously he had been an officer in the cavalry, and consequently there was a lot of criticism and again we struggled to rearrange the various loads more effectively. Finally, we removed the loads, removed the harness, took part in the usual feeding battle, left our animals and went to eat and rest. I suppose that while we in our tents in the smoky atmosphere of an after-dinner cigarette discussed and cursed our mules and their hooves and teeth, the mules themselves at the same time in the fresh air discussed and cursed in mule language the people and their insults and devilry.

The colonel decided that the next day the regiment would march with the mules loaded with all the equipment. We transport soldiers began to work very early to be ready at the arranged time. That day we again had a struggle with the animals, but not as badly as we've learned a few points to more easily get the upper hand.

We finally stood ready in our place, and when every company marched by, their mules followed after them. Soon some of the muleteers were in trouble because of the cunning of the mules. This was the problem. The saddle, on which the loads were hung, was held in position by a belly strap that was set fairly tightly. Well, the cunning mules resisted the tightness of the belly strap. They took a deep breathe and expanded the belly with air while the unsuspecting muleteer fixed the strap. Afterwards the animals let out the air and found the strap much less troublesome. But that loosened the saddle, which gradually moved until finally it suddenly slipped down so the load hung under the belly of the beast between its legs. Of course, the animal immediately became frightened, and of course kicked everywhere with it's hooves, and then galloped away followed by the poor muleteer. Often a lot of things fell out of the load and had to be recovered after the recapture of the mule. Meanwhile, the soldiers who have not been selected as muleteers, enjoyed the joke and laughed loudly.

But this beginning was quite trivial compared with what was to follow. Our bagpipers began to play a Scottish tune, and that was the end. At this all the mules' ears went up, their eyes almost fell out of their heads, their front feet went up in the air, and after a while the valley was full of mules rushing away from the terrifying sounds as if the Devil himself was chasing them. My pair also took part in the panic, but fortunately I held on to them tightly and after a short run, during which I was more in the air than on the ground, they tired and I was able stop them. The musicians saw the effect of their music and so many laughed that the music came to an inglorious end. Less than a quarter of the mules remained on the road. The others were far away on the plain, a lot of them with the loads between the legs, while the perspiring muleteers desperately chased after them. Oh, what a day!!

Those muleteers, who managed to stay with the regiment, returned immediately to the camp, the regiment abandoned their march along the road and walked in a long line across the valley to help capture the mules and recover the lost objects. The same thing happened to all the regiments. We lost some of own mules, but gained some others who belonged to other regiments; so the situation was equalized.

Because of this fiasco, the colonel decided that they should teach the mules to appreciate and love the music of the bagpipes. So, every morning the regimental bandsmen came to the transport section of camp and marched between the mule lines and for half an hour played the tunes they usually played on the march. As we laughed and applauded them mockingly, while the poor mules were completely terrified! We had our revenge for the previous laughter of the bandsmen.

Every night some mules - a lot of them on the first night, before we knew about their cunning and skill - escaped from the mule lines. But they found almost nothing to eat on the plain, and soon found out that it would be wiser to return to the places where they would find food. But understandably they did not find the way to the proper regiment, but to one of the eleven other regiments of the division. So it was a daily (or, rather, nightly) migration. Every morning there was a count of the mules on the lines. If we found more than we ought to have, we smiled. Not because we wanted to have more than we should. Not at all! In fact, it was annoying to have more than the exact number, because someone has to feed and clean more them. So, if there were more than the statutory number, the unwanted would be collect in one place. There they could inspect them to see if among them there were some better, gentler, or tamer than our own. If so, they would be exchanged. When the exchange was completed, the extra mule would be released, and because of strong blows on the back would gallop away to find a more welcoming home. So there was a set of unfortunate untameable mules that went round from one regiment to another. I've even heard of some muleteers who deliberately chased away their mules at night, hoping to thus obtain a peaceful pair.

If on the other hand there were fewer than there should be, then the unfortunate ones who had lost mules had go round other regiments or on to the plain to find any mule. And they knew that probably the mule found would more or less be a wild animal. When the regimental numbers were put on the mules by branding, the game was more straightforward and gradually the mules became accustomed and didn't try to escape.

So, those first days near to Salonika passed with much excitement, and I will never forget the first meeting with our mules. But, little by little, everything became more orderly, the mules became used to the new life, the new work and new objects and sounds around them. At the same time, we have learned much about the mule and his deceit, and soon the mules learned that the rebellion brought them some pain. For example, if they filled the belly with a big breath, it was found that a strong blow in the belly from the muleteer's knee made them let out the air, and that before they could refill the belly, the belly strap was already firmly fixed. Bit by bit, very friendly relations developed between us and our animals.

The first days of our stay on a plain near Salonika were very beautiful. Warmer than the gray October and November days, which we left in the battlefield in France; the atmosphere was warm in view that the month was now December; and the sun was shining brightly. But that lasted only three or four days, and soon after the mules came the rain. It started raining and continued to rain, heavy rain, for a whole week without stopping. We became very miserable.

The 10 December 1916, was a better day. The rain ceased and around noon the sun was warmly shining for one or two hours. In the afternoon, we suddenly received orders to pack our personal things in our backpacks and load our mules. At six o'clock in the evening, we left the camp with the rest of the regiment and started our first long trip with our small collection of friends, the mules. We walked along the road until the midnight hour, passing through neither a town nor even a village; from time to time only a hamlet or secluded house. After a three-hour rest, we again walked as far as the city Topsin, which we reached at 6.30 in the morning. Although somewhat tired, we had to make arrangements for our beasts of burden. To do this, we had to set up stakes firmly in the ground, so that we could fix long ropes between the stakes to which we could tie the mules. While some did this, others unloaded the animals and arranged everything in order, the cooks lit a fire to prepare the ever welcome tea. We watered the animals in a nearby river, where some rolled themselves on the sandy shore; we fed them. Afterwards we were allowed to sit to enjoy the refreshing tea and something to eat. At 7.30 in the morning we dropped off to sleep, and soon silence reigned, except for the noise of the mules, and the weary chatter of those unfortunate ones who had guard duty.

Sometime around noon, they woke us and we found food prepared. Blessed are our cooks! In the afternoon, we cleaned the animals, did some necessary tasks or just laid about idly until the 5 o'clock, when we had to prepare ourselves to go on farther. At six in the evening, we began the journey along the road. Soon we noticed in the lower places the result of the recent heavy rain. Lagoons in fields and rivers that had overflown their banks were frequently noticed.

After some time we found a place where the road seemed to have disappeared into a lake. In every direction there was water and it seemed that there wasn't any other way anywhere on this side of that on which we were travelling. When we had reached that place, I was in the middle of the long column or line of travellers; so I do not know what happened when our officers reached the site. But likely they had met some cavalry men, who explained what had happened and what to do. The road was under the water for a distance of two miles. Not much under the water, only a couple of feet in the worst places. So, we could get through, but we had to remember that the road stands high above the surrounding countryside. So, it is necessary to move forward very carefully so that one didn't go down off the road and be drowned in the deeper adjacent waters. These cavalry men went ahead and stood here and there as mounted sign posts to guide us. When everything was organised, we climbed on the backs of mules, or rather, on the loads, which the poor mules carried.

My mules carried the blankets, which we used during our sleep. For transportation, these were rolled into long, cylinder-shaped packages ten in each package. These packages were hung on the back of a mule, and I think - if memory is reliable - that each mule took a hundred covers, that is ten packages. They were standing on the back of the animal and reached quite high into the air. And I was on the top. Quite comfortable physically - but mentally very unhappy. For my second animal was tied to the saddle of the first on which I am riding and from time to time he went to one side or another, and when this happened it pulled at the saddle on which was my throne and me. I was very afraid that this frequent pulling from side to side would untie my saddle. If this should occur, I would be thrown into the water. But the belly strap remained in its right place, and I remained up there in my high seated position.

The mules proved very wise animals, and advanced slowly, well in the middle of the road. Everywhere around us there was a strange sight. The day comes to an end. The light gradually fades. The district, through which we are travelling, appeared to be empty and almost houseless. From time to time we passed a lonely house, whose lower part you could not see, because it stood in the water. From time to time we passed by the trees standing sadly in a small sea, where there must have been firm ground. However, everything finishes sometime, and without accident we reached the higher ground where there was no water on the road.

The mules and the men were very tired and after a little while, it was decided not to continue to the arranged place, but make camp by the roadside to rest.

The next day, 12th December, we reached Guida, the village, which was our goal from the previous night. There was a railway station where wagons were waiting for us with various necessities. All of which we had to unload and prepare for the continuation of our journey.

We left Guida on the night of the 13th and continued our wanderings for three days. In fact, we rather lost our way and finally were found by a searching unit of cavalry men. We were a day late, and we had already eaten everything. So, we were very pleased when we finally arrived at our destination, the town of Katerini, where the rest of the regiment were, who had reached the place in a warship.

The 18th December, I lost three of my friends. Webster got permission to leave muleteering, Thorne and Marsh had to go to the hospital because of dysentery.

On 19 December, we left Katerini and walked away from the coast to the mountains to a place called Kolokuri, a village near the river Mavroneri. There we found the Kensingtons in various observation posts and defensive positions on the adjacent hills. It seemed that we should wait for the arrival of the feared Greek army to stop its march to the Salonika plain. The transport section of the regiment stayed near the village and did various tasks taking things to the companies on the hills. Those companies, which are not engaged in the hills had to work to strengthen and repair the road, which probably, none of the local residents had maintained.

The days were spent in this way until the 25th, when an attempt was made to arrange some kind of celebration. In the morning, I took a bathe in the nearby river, which in some places was deep enough for swimming. But, although the sun felt quite warm, the water that came from the snowy heights of Mount Olympus was very cold, and we did not stay in swimming for long. Somehow some sheep were acquired, which the chefs cooked for the Christmas Dinner. In addition, we received as a special treat, some of the famous English Christmas pudding. Unfortunately we did not get big portions, because the cooks, having opened the boxes, in some found - not puddings - but sand! Some robber had already seen the chest and had certainly tried our puddings.

That day, the Brigade arranged a great sports competition in Katerini. For those of us on military duty between the hills, we were unable to go to Katerini. Only one quarter of our regiment went there. For those, who remained in Kolokuri, a programme of sporting events was arranged. Among the various games and competitions, a "horse-competition" on mules was arranged. The course was the road up to the top of the slope and back again to the starting point. Many competitors participated, about 40, and my opinion was that it was a very amusing affair – for the onlookers! Many of us were unable to ride and certainly didn't know about horses or animals. The ground on which we rode was somewhat uneven; shrubs grew on it in many places and in some places puddles remained after the rain. Many of those riding fell on the ground and soon only twenty remained of the more experienced of the riders participating. My mule was not very speedy and soon he was only following the leading mules. But I wasn't at all able to control him or guide him. I concentrate completely on my desire to remain seated on his back.

After some time, he went sideways in order to avoid a bush and I went through the air onto the ground in the opposite direction. Fortunately I held the reign and so I didn't lose the mule. I thought of crawling on his back again. This was not easy for I didn't have a saddle or stirrup and the mule didn't want to continue at all. However I finally controlled him and we continued our journey after the others. But I, being completely inexperienced fell to the ground twice more, and soon, after the third fall, I noted that someone had already won the prize, so I unheroically and defeated returned to the camp. I must add, that the following day I found that sitting was not amusing.

In the evening we built a very large fire near the camp, and sat around it singing Christmas carols from the home land. Our padre, Rev. Bruce Nicolls, from time to time told miscellaneous stories and we thus passed a very peaceful and enjoyable evening among the hills of Greece.

Work continued after Christmas. While a few companies from the Brigade were on duty in the advance guard positions on the hills and constructed defence positions, most of them constructed and repaired the road, which wandered in the mountain range high along the valley of the river.

Until the end of the month my company was one of those, who were on duty on the hill and the muleteers, whose mules specially belonged to the company had to go daily, morning and evening, in order to carry the necessities to them. Often when we reached the company, we received another task, which made us go somewhere or other with the loaded mule. There were shrubs on the hills, and I enjoyed the life there very much. The burning line of the cook's fires smelt very pleasant, and even now, when I sometimes smell that kind of odour my thoughts immediately fly to that part of my military service. When we returned to the regimental centre in the evening after the delivery of things to our comrades of the company, we were in the habit of riding on the mules – even though indeed this pleasure was not permitted. Entirely without worrying we left the mule to choose the way while we sat there happily looking at the beautiful surroundings. Everywhere was quiet and peaceful, tranquil. Sometimes one was able to hear the cattle bells, which wandered somewhere between the mountains, sometimes it was possible to see the goats above us on the cliffs, climbing in unreachable, seemingly unreachable places. From lower down, from time to time, one heard sound or shouting from the camp to which we were going. If the weather was good one could see the beauty of the sunset between the clouds and the mountains. In this peaceful atmosphere, I often wandered back to the camp, in a fanciful daydream, until finally I was able to see the light of the regimental cook's fire. Afterwards came that pleasant smell of the wood smoke, which brought thoughts about the desired cup of tea.

Having taken care of the animal, one got the tea at the kitchen, found the tent, crawled in it and in candlelight ate something, had some chat about the day's work, the letters from the homeland, and those kind of things which themselves brought pleasure to the soldiers heart. Finally one extinguished the candle and lay down to go to sleep. The young soldier's possessions lay around in the tent; through the open end of the tent one could see the sky and be astonished about the seeming grandeur of the universe and the peculiar insignificance of the human power.

Often during the night we must do guard duty and care for the mules. It seemed to me, that mules are astonishing animals, apparently never sleep and are always on the move. The regiment's mule herd were stood in four lines, and the animals of every company were tied to a line stretched between stakes. The stakes were covered with metal, because, when we had left them uncovered, the mules next them chewed them, until one stake became broken and immediately afterwards there was a mixed mass of mules and hooves while the mules roamed and fought each other. During the night one was able to hear the movements of the animals, who were very much awake and fighting. Often a mule was able to untie itself from the line and roamed about searching for something to eat. If the one on duty chased him, it galloped away either to right beside the camp or between its comrades, where it was very difficult to capture him.

I remember, that often I passed the whole of a two hour duty chasing mules. This happened in the first days of our experience with the mules. Afterwards we discovered, that a liberated mule has a very good sense of smell when it comes to food, and that every mule, soon after it escaped from the line found its way to the forage store. After this discovery, we took very simple steps; during the night, it became our habit to sit on the forage and just await the arrival of the vagrant! We soon became very expert in the capture of the animals, who without fail were led back again to their line – perhaps with a mouthful of hay –with two or three blows as punishment.

One night a very unpleasant incident occurred to those on duty. They went to sleep and didn't wake until the morning. Meanwhile mules came – and then the regretful men on duty had a terrified feeling, when they awoke. The colonel was furious and punished the offenders severely, not only are they committing one of the worse crime for soldiers – sleeping on the job – but they had allowed the disappearance of the colonel's bran.

On the 5th of January the regiment went forward to Hani Miljas. My company ("D" company) were once again on duty in the hills and each day I continued wandering with the mules. The weather was fine enough, but gradually worsened. The sunny days began to disappear and more clouds came and more rain. The Brigade, of which our regiment was part, was now occupied with the reconstruction of the bridge across the river. The bridge had deteriorated several years before and no one had maintained it, until we, with our military purposes, came and found that the road was seriously interrupted. The bridge was big enough and our engineers sections were very proud of it. It was named Chelsea Bridge, in memory of beloved London, the home of the Brigade.

From about the end of January and in the first half of February, we experienced almost continuous rain. Life became very miserable to every one of us, and especially for us muleteers, everyone of whom seemed to be wet all the time and covered with mud. Also at night it became very cold and often it was difficult to sleep. After awhile some charcoal was found and with it we were able to make a fire in a box to be hung in the tent. This was a comforting discovery – but finally it was banned from use because one soldier forgot to leave a door open in the tent for ventilation and suffocated from the fumes.

On the 13th of February, after completing the bridge, and much more road construction, we marched onwards and upwards. We halted at Petra, a place which is situated 1,000 feet above sea level. The valley of a river lay below, and snaked between the tree covered hills until finally it crossed the plain and reached the sea. When the sun shone and the air was clear, one was able to see the blue of the distant sea. Indeed it presented a beautiful and enjoyable picture to us. The whole place was very similar to parts of Scotland, and because of this touched my heart deeply.

Soon after our arrival, I went with a group of transport men higher as far as Ajos Dimitrios and further as far as the small town of Kokinopolo, where a French detachment was found. This detachment was suffering from lack of nourishment, etc, because the road to the town of the French provision store was obliterated by the rain storms. So we went to them carrying the necessary things. A small detachment of French soldiers went with us for protection as the land across which we must travel was not occupied by ours or other soldiers. I always remember this journey – firstly for the beauty of the landscape, and secondly for the comic appearance of our march. The scenery was beautiful, wild mountains. The river became more and more distant below us. The side of the mountain went more and more sharply down from the road on which we went. The journey was good enough. The French soldiers belonged to some reserve regiment, and for the most part they were amiable enough men. We attempted to be friendly with them, but we completely could not understand each other, and after some time we didn't chat with them anymore. Soon after the start, they marched all over the place. The best marchers went forward rapidly and the others wandered behind according to their ability. Soon the whole detachment stretched over a very long distance on the road. We British were very amused, because we were not allowed to march in such a way. All the time we had to go in neat ranks – of four on the left side of the road, or right, according to the custom of the land on whose roads we were marching. Our colonel would become enraged seeing us march in the manner of those French.

Late in the evening, we reached Kokinpolon, where we were warmly welcomed. We ate with them and received lodgings and gifts of wine. By this I mean, that we resided in barracks instead of in a small tent on wet ground. We soon went to bed so as to very fully enjoy this extraordinary luxury. There we laid in comfort, smoking and playing cards. The town itself appeared big enough, but it had a poor dirty appearance. Understandably we hadn't seen much of it, and possibly it was an entirely good town. I don't know.

The following morning there was very beautiful sunlight and we bid farewell and started travelling again in a very good humour. We found a path across a hill which was a very much shorter way and which also gave us some extremely fine views. Finally we reached the main road, but oh woe! The path on which we had to go in order to reach the main road was very steep and not very usable. It went right downwards towards the road, which was not very wide there; and on the other side of the path the mountainside was nearly vertical for possibly 50 metres down. Both I and some others were not very good riders. However, we had to go along this steep path and I confess, that those two or three minutes during which I went down along the steepest part on my mule were the worst in my life. The mule itself didn't approve of the proposed route and began to go very nervously. Finally, however, everyone of us sliding and sweating reached the road without accident, and again were in some good order. From this place as far as the camp we travelled riding without a care and slowly along the mountain road in the pleasant sunlight.

For me, we didn't stay long enough in this very pleasant mountain home. Early morning, on the 22nd of February, we received the order to pack everything and be prepared to go away somewhere. And soon we were off, marching again along the road which we had just refurbished, across the bridge which was recently constructed. In order to

57

make the day memorable, a rain storm came; an enthusiastically wholehearted rain storm, which lasted all day. We went eighteen miles in five and three quarters of an hours, plus a one hour rest at midday. Perhaps this didn't seem a very astounding task, but one must remember, that there in the Salonika war zone we had to carry the many things for living and protection against the weather. The weight of the equipment and property, which everyone carried was about one hundred pounds - and that is a large enough load for a man to carry anywhere on the march. For the weather there, we must have additional protective clothing. For example, we were given, in addition to our customary clothing, a special jacket made from rough sheep – or goat skin; in addition this was special waterproof surface. As we didn't have any ready-made shelters where we were roaming, everyone had to carry their shelters on their backs in the form of everything required for half of a tent. So we had to live in pairs. These kinds of things were in additional to the customary necessities for a soldier, and as I said before, they made our load very heavy to be carried all the time. So, I believe, that our march again to Katerini was a rather good effort. We camped near Katerini for about two weeks while the chiefs made the necessary arrangements for leaving the place. I forget now, whether some people took the place of us in Katerini; I believeŝ so, but am not sure; we simply formed up, and left the liberated land; supposedly it was decided, that either it wasn't the Greek army or that it wasn't likely to be coming this way.

On the 10th of March, we marched eight miles (12.87 kilometres) as far as Tuzla. On the 11th we went over thirteen miles (20.92 kilo's) as far as Libanovo where we made camp, near a river which soon flowed into the river Vistritza, whose most noteable feature for us were the thousands of gnat and mosquitoes.

After a fourteen mile (22.53 kilo's) march, on the 12th of March, we reached Guilda.

On the 13th, we marched nineteen miles (30.47 kilo's) on the worse road in the world, I believe as far as Topshin.

The following day, we continued the march, but now in a northerly direction to the bank of the River Vardar. That we followed, more or less it, until after 13 miles (12 kilo's) we reached Amatovo. There we passed the night. Until now, although the bad condition of the roads had made our onward march extremely difficult, we had some recompense from the pleasantness of the weather. After the downpours of February on Mount Olympus, the present bright sunny days were very pleasant.

The day which had begun in Amatovo, on the 15th of March, was very fine and warm. We marched some distance until we reach a place called Vardino and halted there in order to rest until nightfall. That afternoon was very enjoyable and were pleasing to us, who were able to rest comfortably on the soft grassy place in the satisfying rays of the warm sun. The life appeared much better than during the recent days.

Finally when it was evening, the order came to prepare ourselves and our animals for the continuation of the journey. After the warm day the evening rapidly became cold. Besides this the wind was beginning to be felt, clouds appeared and soon the night sky was black and menacing. After some time it began to rain. It rained more. Even heavier rain. The rain, driven by the cold wind fell incessantly for hours, while we in melancholic silence marched along the road. The usual singing broke out, and soon even the most enthusiastic good hearted ones hadn't the courage to continue their attempts to make their comrades sing. The weather continued to be awful, we grumbled discontentedly, but the march continued without interruption. When we reached Karasuli, it was said, that we had already finished the journey for this night. The guides spoke to us to show us the place where we must spend the night. I don't know, but probably these guides didn't know the way, and we wandered around at least an hour more, before our guide showed us a very narrow small valley a little above and away from the plain. Water flowed from everywhere in small streams down into the valley and it appeared to us that our comrades from the company would not easily find a place to sleep there. However this wasn't our business. We began to unload our mules and asked for information about our objectives. The captain didn't know. The guide very widely and generally pointed in one direction and said that we should go thence. Then he disappeared completely. So, we went in the direction of his suggestion, and after some time found ourselves on a dirty wet plain. There we found various muleteer comrades from other companies. Where is the transport place? No one knew. Where is the transport officer? Silence! Where is the sergeant? Terrible!! What to do? Now, I and one or two others decided to camp right away, where we were. We wandered around some while searching for some drier piece of ground. But there was none there. Everywhere was only water and mud. We decided not to erect a tent. We tied eight mules into a circle, head to head. Tied in that way, they couldn't wander far. I took the saddle from one of my mules and stood it in the mud so that it could stand as a shelter for my body against the wind. I started to take the saddle from the second mule. Then I noticed newly arriving mules, whose muleteers who marched straight at my saddle lying on the ground and before I was able to remove it, the mules walked across it. I shouted and cursed, but no one paid attention to me. They were all tired and wanting to reach their goal. More and more of them trod my saddle into the mud, until finally I was able to grab it and withdraw it. I set it up again some away from that place, took the second saddle, put it next to the first, put a large cover (which was used to cover the loads of the mules) on the ground; I laid on it, put the second cover over me, and slept despite the heavy rain.

I don't how long I slept, but when I woke up it was full day. I looked around, no movements. What a miserable sight. The sky was full of grey clouds which rushed low across the melancholic plain. Around me the ground was muddy, in several places covered by puddles of dirty water. On this wet ground stood several groups of mules who, amusingly, had an appearance of great misery. I had to laugh, seeing the unhappy faces of our beasts of burden. The muleteers were lying in groups on the mud. Others already stood being very unpleasantly cold. What an awakening! After this I noticed myself. I lay in water. My clothing was all wet down the side

60

on which I laid. Apparently the upper cover had hung immediately next to my body while I slept and consequently the lower one became a container for the water, which flowed from the upper cover. I began to stand up and felt very cold, and decided, that the best method of getting myself warm would be to do something. So, I searched and found my comrade and woke him. We looked for our mules and attempted to clean them, but the mud was too wet and we decided, that the best thing would be to put the saddles on our mules and go to search for the company and there get information about the future. This task of dressing our mules was very difficult, for everything was covered with mud. Nothing could be fixed properly and when we somehow arranged everything, the whole business seemed like a bad comedy and completely unsteady. However, it was possible for us to improve things as the day progressed. After some wandering we again reached the place, where we had left the company in the night. There everyone seemed unhappy and the only good thing about the place was the cooks' smoking fire. These heroic chaps had somehow succeeded in finding wood that was dry enough, and behold they started boiling the water for tea. Soon the tea had been prepared, and with thanks we drank this warm drink, and ate some of the hard biscuits. After the meal, I was ordered to pick up four water containers and to go to search for water. I was given some nebulous information about the place where I will find the water, and without much hope I went off. I was unable to find drinking water, even though I went far enough away; but I told myself, that I couldn't return to the company without water. However, I then met a soldier, who said that was a source of water on the side of some hill which he showed me. Going there, I found a place where mules and horses were taken to drink. I made enquiries, but was unable to find any information about better water. So, I filled the water containers here with the impure water, and carried it back to my comrades.

The morning soon passed during which we worked, and after the midday meal we had some rest, passing the time by attempting to remove some of the mud. By evening we began work again, preparing ourselves and our mules for the nocturnal march. Again the sky was covered with grey clouds, which went more and more rapidly, while a stronger and stronger cold wind blew. The march was begun and we cheered up, because this marching began to make us warm. We went 15 miles (24 kilo's), which wasn't easy, not only because of the bad road, but also because of the fact that the wind blew strongly straight across our road. Finally, we reached Kalinova, in some hilly location. We unloaded the mules and erected our tents. I lived with my comrade Bert Golding from Banbury, a good-hearted countryman. We were quick, for we were tired, and because of our desire to get some shelter against the sharply chilling wind. And really it was fortunate that we did this, for before we had crawled into our lodgings, it began to snow. And while we slept the snow fell until there were several inches of snow everywhere on the ground.

When we woke in the morning, we found ourselves in a white world between a group of hills. And actually we had already reached our objective. We stayed here for some time. Why? At that time we didn't know; but that is another story. As the morning passed, we heard that some of the regiments were caught in the snow storm before they reached their objective and some mules and one man perished because of the cold. Fortunately, that night our regiment was the first of the Brigade and because of this missed the worst part of the storm. We had erected our tents when there wasn't any snow on the ground. The other unfortunate ones had to remove the snow before that they were able to lay themselves down to sleep.

So, we had experienced a very difficult march. From Katerini to Kalinova was 94 miles (151 kilometres). We did this journey in six days, on very bad roads, carrying very heavy loads on our backs, and in atrocious weather during the last two days.

The total number of men, who didn't finish the journey on their feet was 15, of whom 2 seriously ill and two suffer from an accident. That last savage night, one of our comrades fainted and died on the journey before medical assistance could be brought.

On the 17th of March we looked around; our regiment had put in things ready for occupying the location. Meanwhile we met soldiers from the regiment who we found there already and learnt from them, that the battle line here was on the hill, that the enemy were Bulgarians, that the weather in the recent passed months was awfully severe, and many of the men became ill and some died from the bad living conditions. An encouraging welcome, wasn't it?

The following day, our regiment replaced the 11th Scottish Rifles in the reserve position at Dâche. The other regiments to be found there were:- Queen's Westminster and Civil Service Rifles who went into the battle line, while the Kensingtons were the support line.

The part of the line held by the 60a Division (our division) stretched from the south eastern hills of the mountain chain known as the Pip Ridges, and went eastwards across broken hilly land as far as the valley of the river Vardar, where the British division made contact with the French. The line of the 179a Brigade (our brigade) on the left flank of the division, laid between the lower side of the mountain called Whaleback and the village of Little Berkerli. Two regiments occupied the battle line, the third was in the support line and the fourth in reserve.

We, in the London Scottish, were at first in the reserve and were located in a comfortable sheltered place beside Dâche on the rear flank of the hill, north of Kalinova village.

The army's defensive system was incomplete. The first line was nearly complete, but it needed further strengthening. The support lines were only half built, and the reserve line was even less prepared. To us in the reserve position, were given the task to complete this third line, and to build the intercommunication trenches for the whole system.

Our regiment already had a variety of skills related to building trenches in other places; but the work here was more heart breaking, than sometimes we remembered. The ground, in which we must build the trenches, consists of two or three inches of soft ground and, under this, there is solid rock. The only effective means is to use explosive. By day small holes were made in the rock, at dusk the explosive was exploded and by night the loose rock was dug out. Such work was very difficult and tiring. Besides, the progress was slowed by the fact, that only the engineering soldiers were permitted to use the explosives firing mechanism. Often we found, that the explosion didn't work properly, but we weren't able to do anything except to wait the arrival of the engineers the next evening. Certainly, when this occurred, we personally passed an easy night, but we really did not appreciate the delay very much, for one heard about the expected big Bulgarian attack.

One day, the 29th of March, 1917, I sent a letter home to my young brother. (Understandably, this is not the only one which I sent, but only one from the few of those remaining after the war). It was not permissible to give the exact address.

> *Salonika Army*
> *Thursday, 29-3-17*
>
> *Dear Dave,*
> *Finally I am replying to your last letter. I am very well, thank you, and very pleased to read that those at home are also well.*
>
> *I suppose, that you enjoyed good sport in the snow while it lasted. We had some snow here at the end of January, but now the snow is a thing far from our thoughts. Already the weather is like middle of summer and, because of this, we all feel very lazy. At present, our machine gun section does nightly duty in the reserve trench; so during the day we rest. So for sometime, I have ceased to be a muleteer and now act as a machine gunner again. I don't know which I prefer, for both have their own special interest. But it is good to be among my old comrades again.*
>
> *At present we appreciate being here, for here we find many strange beasts. Among them, some diverse species of snakes; some of these are venomous. Also we see tortoises and lizards, in large numbers. Often under the rocks there are many strange insects, from our point of view amongst*

these the most serious are the scorpions. These are dangerously venomous and because of this we must be very cautious when we move rocks, when we dig trenches, or especially when we build shelters from rocks.

Near our camp is a swamp, and in this are thousands of frogs and toads. They croak loudly all through the night. A very loud and strange sound. One can't imagine that such a din could come from toads and frogs. But there are probably thousands of them. When I first heard this sound, I was very astonished by it, and didn't understand where it came from.

I could describe many such things, which are unfamiliar to the English, but we must wait until the Germans surrender and we are able to return home.

I am trying to collect some Greek coins for you, and now have ten of these to be sent to you. I expect that you now have a good enough collection.

I enjoy reading, that your collection of animals are living happily. Presumably you are able to sell some of your baby rabbits.

Tell Dad, that I have sent the letter to Jim Crawford, and that I shall soon write to him myself. The package, to which you allude, hasn't come yet, but we now are waiting to receive a large delivery of post in the coming two days. We don't receive our letters regularly; but large numbers of letters and packages arrive every week.

Loving greetings to Annie, Edie and Dad. Does Miss Russell sometimes visit you now? Pass on my greetings to her when you next see her.

Hoping to receive a letter soon, I remain
Your loving brother
Robin

On the 3rd of April, we left our shelters beside Dâche and went to relieve the Queen's Westminsters. We were warned to be especially alert because of the fact that the Bulgarians, who were experts in mountain warfare, had by surprise already captured the whole position of the Queens Westminster, without much trouble or struggle. Because of the fact that there existed a long enough distance between their most forward position and the adjacent positions, this was an easy enough matter.

The piece of the battle line, which our regiment defended, stretched from the lower part of the Whaleback Hill, across the intervening valley and upwards and afterwards across Bowls Hill. The trench line itself was dug well enough, but a little too shallow. Also a wide strip of wire was laid for protection, and extended along the whole length of the line. The land in front of us, beyond a gully, went upwards along a noticeable gradient as far as the Bulgarian positions on the Pip Ridges, which overlooked our position. Behind the Pip Ridges, the well known Mountain 535 stood very high. This famous point, on which there was an observation post, capable of looking across the whole of the British position. It wasn't easy to find a place, anywhere between the line and Salonika, from which one couldn't see Mount 535. And all the time during the day, one felt, that the eye of an observer on that point followed every movement. About halfway between the British and the Bulgarian lines laid the uninhabited village named Krastali.

One place, where one was able to move from the view of the "eye" on Mountain 535 was behind Bowls Hill, on which our company was on duty. There we camped. During the day, most of the company slept, rested and ate, or carried out urgent duties for that day. At the same time, a few of us had to sit in the shallow trenches to observe the activity (if any) in the valley or on the opposite mountain, where supposedly the Bulgarians were doing the same. This duty was an unpleasantly tedious business. One wasn't able to move much, for, because of the lack of shelter, any movement was soon observed from the "eye". And any noticeable movement brought a gift in the form of a well aimed shell sent from our neighbours.

There was an interconnecting trench between the first line and the company command position, but also it wasn't very deep and also at the same time under the continuous observation from that accursed Mountain 535. From the company office to the rear it was necessary to go at ground level, and because of this one could only go back and forth at night. The supporting company was approximately 500 yards behind the first line at Worcester Post and the regimental office was at Crow Hill.

At night, most of those, who weren't on duty during the day, went to occupy the defence posts, and those companions who were in them during the day, returned to stretch their legs, drink warm cups of tea and go to sleep. Meanwhile, the others guarded the line and tried to dig deeper in the hard earth.

The second night of our remaining in these trenches there was an occasional bombardment on the right flank of our regiment. After this, every evening we sent groups of men outside the protecting wire on observation patrol. Around midnight, on 6th of April (Holy Friday) the Bulgarians vigorously bombarded our positions with howitzers. This bombardment put our telephone equipment out of action, because of this we couldn't ask for a retaliating bombardment from our artillery. Under the cover of this bombardment, approximately forty enemy attacked the patrol of our right hand neighbouring company. The patrol, which consisted of one officer and sixteen others, responded with rapid fire, which halted the enemy's advance. Afterwards there was occasional exchange of fire, but no further attack, and afterwards the attackers left, leaving three dying. Our patrol lost one dead and six wounded.

After this failure, the enemy was unable to make more of those adventures; we on our side, weren't prepared to attack the fortifications of the Bulgarians, and the line therefore became very calm and peaceful.

Meanwhile, we did night duty and rested by day – except those days when we had to be in the trenches in order to observe. The trenches got deeper and deeper and so the day duty became more tolerable. While we rested there in the day, we had sufficient time to look around. The view was much more interesting, much more extensive and much more worth seeing than that, which we had seen serving in posts in the French countryside. There we were only able to see a dirty mixture of mud, wire and other rubbish between the weeds in the immediate surroundings; and beyond that only flat areas on which there were a few partly destroyed trees, some ruined houses and grey looking heaps of hay. But here in a place in Macedonia, our post was on the side of a hill. In front of us as far as one's eye can see, lay mountains in every direction, with that accursed 535 above everything away to the right.

A few trees grow on the mountains; in several places there were only a few shrubs. On one hill near us was a solitary tree, and because of this we named the hill Single Tree Hill. In the valley and on our hill some varied coloured spring flowers grew.

As regards the enemy positions, we weren't able to see much, even using binoculars. Supposedly the reason is that, because of the rough rocky nature of the top of the hill, one couldn't only see the rocks, which presumably had been dug out constructing their trenches. And similarly the Bulgarians couldn't see our positions, if we didn't make ourselves visible through our movements, or provided they didn't send an aeroplane over to observe us in detail.

I remember, that we were able to see roads behind the Bulgarian trenches, which came across the shoulder of one mountain and disappeared behind another nearer hill. One evening, I noticed something moving on this road. The binoculars revealed to my sight a group of transport animals. From the rangefinder I found, that the road was beyond the firing limits of our machine gun. That night I reported the matter to our officer, who informed the artillery. But, although I often saw these evening transport columns, only very infrequently did I notice any bombardment of the place.

Supposedly, our army didn't have enough ammunition for this relatively unimportant target.

During the night, apart from the frogs and toads, from time to time various birds and animals were heard; these abrasive melancholic cries sounded very alarming in the night's silence. A few times, while patrolling between the two positions, one such bird suddenly flew up from a place immediately nearby, and crying noisily, flew away. Such things were somewhat scary, and one felt one's heart jumped into one's mouth. Although life on the ground was peaceful enough, in the air almost continuous activity took place. The enemy aeroplanes were very active and much stronger and numerous than ours. Very often they flew across us to visit the town of Salonika, the camps, munitions dumps, and provision stores in order to drop bombs on them. Others flew over us in order to observe and photograph our positions, and from time to time throw bombs on us or fire at us with machine guns.

These enemy aeroplanes also came in order to attack our observation balloons, which every day during daylight hung in the air in to watch the enemy lines as much as possible. These balloons represented the attempt of our army to set up something for watching the enemy in a manner similar to that by means of which he watched us by means of the "eye" on mountain 535. The balloon was tied to a machine on the ground with which it could be put up for observation, or returned to the ground in times of danger or when the duty was finished. The man who worked in the balloon, must be always be prepare to escape and come to the ground by his parachute. Probably these balloons disturbed and angered the enemy very much, because very often he was able to destroy them by an aeroplane attack. But this was also a dangerous adventure for the attackers, because our anti-aircraft artillery was very skilled. They set their aim, so that if an attack occurred, they fired at some point through which the aeroplane must certainly fly. In this manner, several aeroplanes were destroyed during an attack; not infrequently both the aeroplane and the balloon fell together at the same time. The method of the attack was for the aeroplane to come from high in the air downwards to the balloon; when the attacker was above the balloon, he fired with a machine gun, whose bullets penetrated the balloon and ignited the gas. Then the observer had to escape with his parachute, at the same time hoping that burning balloon didn't fall on him.

Subsequently the enemy aeroplane found a good way to avoid destruction. They went high in the air, and, when in a good position, they stopped the engine and made a fall towards the balloon. This way one didn't notice their arrival until one heard the sound of the machine gun fire and the restarting of the aeroplane while it flew away. On one occasion I saw such an attack, and I greatly admired the great courage and skill of the aviator.

After some time a group of British aviators came into the Salonika region, who were much more courageous and much more skilled than the enemy. Then there were views of aerial battles on many occasions. Both nations had successes, but bit after bit the British won, and once again the air became more favourable to us on the ground.

On the 21st of April, our artillery began a very steady bombardment of the enemy positions on the Pip Ridges, to the right of our position. We saw the shells exploding there on the mountains. And we wondered about the significance of this unusual ferocity. We heard, that the British intended to make a large-scale attack against these fortified positions, and that we must be prepared to intervene in a push forward if this attack succeeds. The bombardment continued for a week. On the 24th April the attack started. It continued until the 28th when the last big struggle occurred. The attack was almost totally unsuccessful. Some less important gains were little profit compared to the large loss of men. The positions on top of the heights were too inaccessible and, apart from this, the enemy alerted by the long bombardment, greatly increased the number of defenders in the positions.

In the meanwhile, on the 25th of April, we changed our position, going a little to the left in order to replace the Queens Westminsters. Our new home consisted of two hills, 275 and P6. On both we found well made trenches. In the valley, between the two hills, was very strong wire protection.

By night we sent very strong patrols there and back between the two hills. The hillside, which faced towards the enemy positions, was very steep and easily defendable against attack. On the lower ground, in front of our positions, grew dense and long lush grass. On this grassy area, we patrolled every night, from time to time exchanging bullets and bombs with our Bulgarian 'friends'. Behind this lower place, lay a chain of the hills in the middle of the wide "no-man's land". According to the map, these had no names. So we christened them Turtle Back, Pigeon, Single Tree, Tomato and Lancaster.

After the failure on the Pip Ridges, it was decided, that our division should push forward our own line to occupy part of the quite wide strip of ground between ours and the Bulgarian lines. To us, the idea seemed rather risky and valueless. For the new line (if we should succeed to capture and hold it) will be a less easily defendable position than the present one, and apart from that, it was in a place more easily bombarded by the enemy.

At first, the 180a Brigade attempted to capture the prominent enemy position called The Nose. This attack failed. Afterwards our Brigade (the 179a) as ordered to prepare to try to begin to occupy the selected part of "no-man's land". On the 5th of May, we began to carry forward to a place in front of our line the various things needed, in order to hide them there, in readiness for the coming work. We did this for three nights, and began to know well the night time appearance of this place. These manoeuvres weren't without excitement, for from time to time, the patrols met the Bulgarian patrols and exchanged the customary unfriendly greetings.

Finally, on the evening of the 8th of May, the actual forward movement began. At 8.15, my section went forward and finally, with the rest of our company, lay down a little in front of the position, which our regiment had been ordered to occupy. Soon some kind of Bulgarian patrol came and received a hostile reception from us. After some firing, they left. Another of their patrols had the same experience on another part of the front, and apparently sent a report back to their superiors; because after some time, a heavy bombardment of the place, where we and the rest of the regiment was working, began. The Bulgarians very systematically sought us with their shells. We noticed, for example, that one battery fired in the same direction, and extended the firing distance each time by about 50 yards. These shells came in our direction, and every time we saw them come closer and closer. Finally, when they reached the point at which we thought that the following salvo would hit us, we went forward 100 yards and happily noticed that the shells this time fell behind us. Through this observation and intelligent foresight, our officer undoubtedly avoided some unpleasant deaths.

While we ventured forward in that way to stop any attack against our new position, the others worked hard on the hills. They constructed a strong defensive system with barbed wire, and dug some sort of trench system. When day came, we went back to the old line. We left small groups in the new positions, in order to defend them from any daytime attack.

In the night of the 9th May, we continued our work on the newly occupied hill. That day, a Bulgarian aeroplane was flying across our new positions. Supposedly they reported the fact and probably the Bulgarians thought that our activities were not very serious, for the next two nights, they didn't bombard us much. The work made good progress during the night, and when it was day we were close to achieving our desired objective.

On the night of the 10th of April (?May), the first serious attack occurred against our division in the new position. The Bulgarians attacked the Westminsters position; they killed every one of the defenders and captured the position. The Westminsters immediately retaliated and recaptured the position.

About midnight, another regiment (Civil Service Rifles) came to replace us, and we went back to the reserve position. During this manoeuvre, our regiment lost thirty comrades, dead and wounded; and after some time the newly gained positions were left as useless. Was it a wise strategy?

After this fighting, we went to the reserve position at Tertre Verte. We had been on duty in the battle line for thirty eight days, and we relished the chance to go into a much less dangerous place, where we were able to wash ourselves and to receive clean underwear, and rest in a more peaceful and stress free atmosphere.

The weather now became very warm during daytime, and, because of this, we didn't like working much, and were very pleased with the rest which we experienced during the two or three days immediately after our return from the battle line. But afterwards we had to do a lot of work, just as normal when in a "rest". Understandably, most of it had to be done at night because of the observation position on Mountain 535. So, most of the regiment slept during the day and worked at night.

However we machine gunners didn't do this, for we received special tasks. Firstly, we had to instruct several newcomers in the use of the gun. We had lost several comrades in the previous days and had to welcome new comrades into the section. It was possible to do this instruction safely near the tents. Secondly, we had to do duty with the gun during the day in order to watch for the enemy aeroplanes, and fire if they came too low over our camp. Although the air was mainly controlled by our airmen, at the same time the enemy often sent aircraft in order to bomb our camp and provision stores.

On the hill in or near the place where our regiment lay in their tents, stands were set up on which we fixed our gun so that, we could, if necessary, fire in into the air in any direction. During the day, we were on duty, sitting near the stand, ears alert listening. When an aeroplane was heard, one must search the sky in order to find it; use the binoculars to discover whose it is "ours" or "theirs" and to follow it by eye until it disappeared. If it was an enemy and came close enough, and if our firing would not endanger our comrades from our own falling bullets, in these circumstances we had to fire. It was a nice comfortable task, which we found very satisfying, for while we did this, the other comrades worked quite hard. Two or three times we had to fire at a visiting aeroplane. I don't know whether we hit any of them – there is no doubt that at no time did we bring any down.

On the 20th of May, laying in my own bivouac, I again wrote to my father.

Salonika Army
Sunday, 20th May 1917

Dear Dad
Just a few lines to tell you of my well being here. I am in very good health. In fact I am so well, that my appetite is much too big for the quantity of food I get. Although we receive some large meals, as much as in any other time in my soldier's life apart from in England, I find it a difficult to keep tomorrow's food until the morning.

Our group of comrades in the machine gun section find enough pleasure in the life. I dare to say, that we are one of the happiest in the regiment. We often succeed in getting compliments for our work from the company captain. It is our corporal who sets a high standard and makes us attain it. He is a brave one, who is certainly well acquainted with our Lewis machine gun, which we call "mouth". He is Findlay, intimately called "Bill". He has a fine sweet singing voice and is accustomed to start our evening sing-song. I have to tell you, that we completely enjoy our own attempts to make harmonious music. We are very skilled singers of hymn tunes, and as our accompanist, Sergeant Rookes, helps us with his mouth organ, the general effect is very good.

Our number 2 in the section is soldier Brinson, who answers to the name of "Burny". He is a comedian, who, before the war, sometimes performed as an actor and sometimes sang. I assure you, that he really enlivens our circle. When he and I argue, I called him a "red nosed comedian" and he retorted by calling me a "black fuzzy wuzzy".

Our Number 3 is John Bullock, usually called – John. He was also a comical youngster, whose main hobby is the collection of military memorabilia. He already has about twenty of these, and often adds new specimens to his collection. I admire his enthusiasm, which causes him to carry some of these unnecessary items in the knapsack.

I am Number 4 in the section.

Number 5 is Soldier Vivian Marsh, whose parents live in the county of Devon, where they cultivate the land. By night, in our dugout shelter, we often vigorously discussed and debated the state of life in the home land. Some of us were unfavourable towards the agriculturalists and said that they are not very good in fulfilling their task of feeding the nation. Understandably Vi Marsh very angrily opposed this and we pass the time in this very amusing way. In fact, sometimes he is "like a fish out of the water" in the rough army life, I believe that he is the only son of his mother who brought him up very delicately. However, he has now got used to it and is a good soldier and likeable comrade. The other comrade, who encourages these debates about agriculture, is our sixth member, Bert Golder from Banbury, in the county of Oxford. He is the son of a farm labourer and strongly supports the point of view of our Devon comrade. I first met him in the transport section, when we first received the mules. He and I travelled together and occupied the same tent. He is also a very good tempered helpful comrade, whom I greatly esteem.

Our seventh comrade is soldier Clifton. He is an artist, who draws very well. He has already made very good portraits of several of us, and I hope he will also do mine. When he does this, I will send the portrait home to keep as a memento. Meanwhile, I am living in a fine tiny dugout, which is big enough to hold everyone of us – all seven. Immediately after our arrival in the new camp, we start to find and collect wooden boxes, pieces of wood and much more, and soon we are building a cupboard, shelves, hooks, etc. In our new dugout, we have a shell case, which we use as a vase to hold flowers. We also use a small tin box for the same purpose, and we collect fresh flowers daily.

At the present moment, Bert Golding and Clifton are preparing soup for our evening meal. They are using an old tin box as a cooking pot which they hold over a fire made from some of the pieces of wood. One result from this military experience is that later we will be good cooks.

At present we are passing a very easy time. We are now away from the battle line for a rest period and doing some very interesting exercises. One day we did firing practice. On the firing range were a rank of targets, whose shape represented lying men; behind them were other targets which represented other men running forward to support the others. These latter targets remained standing while we fired at the others and remained standing for some seconds and afterwards disappeared. Our platoon succeeded in gaining the most points, and this fact made us very happy. We passed another day with machine gun practice. This time I succeeded in proving that I still retained my skill with the gun, even though I hadn't used it during the time in the hills in my "career" as a muleteer. The whole business was enormously interesting and I really enjoy when we have the chance to do this type of exercise.

Yesterday was one of our unlucky days. We had to keep digging the whole day. The rest of the company enjoyed two days of free time. Between 11 in the morning and 3 in the afternoon, it was too hot to work and we had this time for a long rest. You would have been laughing at us when we had to push the handcart across the river on a narrow wooden bridge. There wasn't nearly enough width to walk easily, and the small handcart certainly wasn't much help to us, and we were in constant danger of falling into the water. However everyone of us very successfully avoided this fate.

Today we had the pleasure of enjoying a warm bath. The engineers of the division very cleverly arranged for the heating of water and arranging for it to be suddenly tipped through holes in the ceiling of the place onto us. We, with soap in hand, stood there naked and washed ourselves while the water remained warm. This was a very luxurious affair and we were very thankful to those who arranged the

apparatus. After this bath, the doctor closely examined us.
Sometimes a day was very lazy and enjoyable and today in
the evening we feel very happy and after the meal of some
soup (or some other drinks), which was cooked by Bert and
Cliff, we undoubtedly sang well and happily.

> *We are waiting to soon go into the battle line again, but*
we don't reliably know anything.

> *Now, I can't write any more, but will finish with*
greetings to all of you. Oh, that reminds me! Have you at some
time received a postcard, which I sent you from Marseilles?
> *Please inform me about this when you write to me.*
> *How are David's animals?*
> *Love from your son,*
> *Bob*

The day after writing this letter, this was the 21st of May
1917, once again we went into the battle line. But now this was
peaceful enough. The weather was much warmer than during
our previous spell there and the daily duty of lookout in the line
by oneself was not a very pleasant task.

Because of the warmth and in order to avoid, as far as
possible, malaria fever which often attacked our soldiers in
that battle field, before long they began to give us doses of
quinine from time to time. The distribution of these doses
was a very amusing business. Usually this happened in the
evening just before we went from the camp to the other side
of the hill for the nightly duty in the line. The sergeant of
every platoon received enough quinine for his men, from the
regimental doctor. He parades us and, one after another, we
must receive from him some of the quinine in a cup and drink
it. Understandably, because of the bitter taste, we disliked it,
and a number of times (rather like naughty boys) it was spat
on to the ground instead of being drunk. The whole business
seemed to me as if a large family of boys, who had been eating
green apples, and who had received unpleasantly tasting
medicine from their mother, partly as punishment and partly
to take away the painful result of their wrong doing. And the
sergeant was the angry mother, who looked severely at every

sinner to make a note of them, so that none evaded punishment.

One evening, when the sergeant was giving some of the quinine to all of his soldiers, some remained in the jug. He announced with a smile that anyone, who wishes to try, could drink the rest. Much to our surprise, one of our comrades accepted the offer and drank a quite a large quantity. Afterwards, when we were on duty in the line, this man felt very unwell. As if inebriated, but with a very painful head. He was totally unable to work and very soon was unable to stand. Finally, he felt so ill, that it was decided that it would be preferable to send him back again into the camp. Because he couldn't walk properly, a comrade must go with him. We heard later, that this journey was a very exciting business, and came to an end when the sick man fell on the tent of two doctors, who were asleep in it. They awoke thinking, that this was some enemy attack and took hold of their guns prepared for a fight to the death. Fortunately, the guide for the sick man cried out loudly in order to stop the probable murder. Then the doctors came out of the collapsing thing, and, cursing in a grumpy way, started to re-erect their tent. The accompanying guide finally brought his comrade into his own tent, where he had to lie until the morning, when he was able to be brought to the doctor.

On the 26th May, I sent a letter to our youngest brother, who was still at school.

Salonika Army
26th May 1917

My dear David
Many thanks for your letter, which had arrived some days ago. I am sorry to read that your Easter holiday was a washout. Hopefully Whitson is more pleasant. Here the weather is very hot and the mosquitoes are starting to bother us. My present opinion is that even the changeable weather of England is preferable. How does the garden look at this time? Supposedly it now contains vegetables instead of flowers in order to help the nation, which is lacking some food stuffs.

I have about twelve coins for you – including from Greece, Italy, Argentina and an Australian sixpence.

After the time when I sent the letter to Dad, we were going to move and now we find ourselves in the line again.

Tell Annie that I am waiting for a letter from her and hope to soon receive the parcel, which she has sent. Supposedly I must await at least one month more; calculating from the time which the last one took to reach me.

I am happy to be able to say that I am still feeling well. How are you all feeling? Well I hope. Are arrangements to be made for a sports day at the school in the New Year? I think that it must be very difficult for the small number of teachers to do the necessary work; especially now when most are women.

And now I must stop, for this is the last piece of paper. I would be able to write much longer letters if I could receive a much bigger quantity of paper.

With greetings and love to everyone,
I remain lovingly yours
Robin

One day I was on duty in the line in the day time. I heard the sound of an aeroplane in the air somewhere behind our line. Afterwards, came the sound of exploding bombs and the noise of the aeroplane becoming extremely loud. Apparently it was very near. Yes, here it is coming over the mountain. Very low. It presented a good target at which to fire. At once and without thought I snatched my machine gun and began to fire. My aerial friend really didn't like my attempts, and accelerated his flying machine, at the same time dropping a bomb on me. I heard a very, very short whistling sound, and then my world shook in a very large explosion. It appeared that the world disintegrated and flew everywhere. The air vibrated from the noise, the air was full

79

of dust, and the acrid smoke and gas made by the explosion. Then stones and rocks fell from the air hitting me on my body. Fortunately my steel helmet remained on my head, and this protected me from serious damage. Understandably, this occurred in two or three seconds and then I knew, that I wasn't dead, but still alive. I wasn't able to hear anything, but I looked away into the air for the enemy aeroplane. The aviator was then going home, supposedly of the opinion, that he had killed the devilish Briton and broken their machine gun. But he was wrong for I found that, except for two or three painful bruises and a sharp head ache I was not damaged. And my friend, the machine gun wasn't broken – only terribly dirty from the stones and dust.

I now explored to find where the bomb had fallen, and found a very big hole in the rock about two or three yards from where I was. It was a miracle that I was still alive. The trench had been made with a bend and the bomb fell in it, so that there were two or three yards of rock between me and it. This saved my life. The explosion severely shook me, and I felt somewhat miserable for some time, but I wasn't able to rest. I must at once clean my machine gun and remain ready to observe from my lookout post. Soon, however, the head ache went away and I was able to hear again, and after some time everything became normal.

On the 3rd June, the commanding General from a neighbouring division came to inspect our part of the line. He congratulated our colonel for the good quality of the defence system and the cleanness of the trenches. This visit, stimulated various rumours about forthcoming movements, and this time the prophets were right. The following evening the Argyll & Sutherland Highlanders (12th Battalion) came to replace us; and we went away to the shelter at Dâche, where we had resided when we first came into this part of the battlefield.

When we were in Dâche it was heard we will definitely be leaving this part of the line, but not even a very smallest detail about our new objective was to be heard. In the meantime, we carried out exercises trying new manoeuvres and methods of attack.

On the evening of the 8th June, when it became dark, the regiment paraded, prepared to leave, and marched to an assembly point near the railway station at Kalinova. No one knew where we were going. The brigade marched off,and soon went south. We marched the whole night. When day came, we made camp near Vergetor. Afterwards we continued the march and passed by Sarigol on the 9th of June; Ambarkeni on the 10th; Naresh on the 11th; and when day came we went forward as far as Uchantur, three miles to the east. Here we found that a great army camp had already been set up. Here we were to reside.

One couldn't get permission to visit Salonika and one didn't hear anything about the future move. But soon we noticed that from time to time various regiments marched in the direction of Salonika and didn't return. Meanwhile, we did many diverse exercises. Two or three times we experienced very exciting interruptions in our exercises. Most of the fear from these was because of the information that the Bulgarians are preparing to make a gigantic air attack on Salonika. To begin with, it was ordered that when the alarm signal is heard, the whole regiment should cease whatever it is doing and should run from the camp, onto the nearby plain, and disperse into small groups. But this manoeuvre caused so much dust in the air, that it presented good information about our stratagem to the attacking airmen. Afterwards it was decided that we should dig trenches as shelters for use during an air attack. So, we again received some more practice in this exercise. And we again found hard ground, which very slowly yielded to our attack with steel spades and separators. we worked for eighteen hours in order to reach the desired depth. And the air attack never happened.

The second excitement was a sand storm. Some afternoon, Saturday or Sunday, I believe, we were lying in our bivouacs chatting, singing or dosing. We were no longer were in the big camp, as we were sent away from there when it was heard about the supposed air attack. Suddenly, in the middle of calm bright sunny weather, the wind began to blow strongly.

And to our surprise the air became filled with sand. Rapidly the wind grew stronger and stronger, and the air filled with more sand, so breathing became difficult and troublesome. One side of the tent began to flap in the wind, but one of us caught it and tied it in its place. Every one of us held some part of the home to prevent it flying away. It was very dark. The gale continued for twenty minutes, and then afterwards it began to rain. I can't remember a heavier rain storm. After two or three minutes, streams flowed down from the hillside. While we knew that the home was in danger of being blown away, we also knew of the danger from the water threatening it. After the rain free weather following our arrival, we hadn't dug drainage trenches around our home and the water began to come in. What to do? In this rain all would soon be soaked; if we remained in the tent everyone would be soaked. I had a good idea. Why not undress ourselves and go out. This would have two benefits; firstly we would be able to save the home without making our clothes wet; secondly the rain will wash away the sand from our skin, which had penetrated everywhere. So, we rapidly followed this suggestion and were soon digging the protective trench around our home. Soon other nudes appeared from other tents in order to do the same. Afterwards, we danced around in the rain, which was very refreshing.

Not everyone in the regiment were as fortunate as us. Many of them had their personal belongings outside the home when the wind began to blow. Soon these objects – hats, shirts, kilts, woollen coverings, joined the procession from the camp, over the cliff, into the sea. Even one or two tents blew away, among these the office tent of one of the companies. When it fell, a mass of paper and documents appeared flying away, which joyfully competed with the other objects to reach the open sea.

On the 29th of June, the order came to be prepared to leave, and at about 2 o'clock in the morning, on the 30th of June. We paraded and marched to the dock in Salonika. There we went by boat to the transport ship H.M.T. Aragon, which laid in the outer part of the harbour. Everyone of us were on the ship by 8 o'clock in the morning. We stayed in the harbour the whole day while other soldiers came onto the ship.

While we stayed there, we were able go round the ship in order to see what it was like. It was a typical transport ship for soldiers; totally different from the luxurious "Megantic" in which we had travelled from Marseilles to Salonika seven months ago. On the lower decks, we found rough tables and benches. We discovered that there weren't any cabins in which to sleep. We had to lie on or near the tables.

On this ship we left Salonika at 8 o'clock in the evening for the journey to Egypt to continue our adventures, this time into the mysterious orient.

Chapter IV

Egypt And Palestine

On the 30th of June 1917, we left the Greek harbour of Salonika. The transport ship "Aragon" continuing to follow its route across the blue Mediterranean, and tried to accomplish its difficult task to transport its brave human load carefully and accurately through the Greek archipelago. It had to avoid getting too close to these unnamed islands, and to cautiously find the way through these waters, which concealed many German submarines whose aim was to find English victims. The weather was perfect compared with the standard of what we had experienced during the past months. It was late morning and as we looked out across the mass of deep blue water, wondering, there appeared, as if from nowhere and slightly veiled with a opal like gauze, a very beautiful island with sharp indented cliffs.

We were ordered to carry our lifejackets and go bare footed during the voyage, and this we did unwillingly, although after a while it was very uncomfortable because of the sun's strong rays, which heated every part of the deck very much. The ship was uncomfortably full, so that by night, everything, even the smallest piece of the deck was cover with sleeping humanity; but grumbling for what reason, are we not going to the Orient, the mysterious sunlit Orient?

Every one of us was full of that feeling of expectation, that even ordinary humans experience when they are approaching a foreign land. Two days ago, the speculators in the regiment predicted that we will be going to Egypt, but then most of them did not know how true their prediction was, and certainly none of them even dreamt, that we would go there by the way of Vimy Ridge, Mount Olympus and Macedonia. Except for the one day that we entered the harbour of Mudras, in order take on board a few unhappy individuals who were on a recently sunk transport ship, we experienced a very pleasant voyage. I well remember the surprise I had when I saw the large hidden sheltered area behind the entrance, which appeared as though a large ship would not be able to enter. There were several Italian battleships, and the crew loudly greeted us with "Hip, Hip, Hurrah". One simply couldn't image that such a place existed.

After the first day of our voyage, when we had just left the Greek Archipelago, we began to see a large group of dolphins now several metres ahead of the ship. It appeared as though they had taken on the task of guarding us, for all the time they persistently went ahead if us, now on one side of the ship, afterwards on the other side. One could image that it was they, and not the two alert escort ships who are responsible for our safety. On the ship, our soldiers passed the time in a variety of ways. Some military activities were arranged, for example, physical exercises, guard duties, work. But even so there was plenty of time left free for us. We passed this time by playing cards until we were bored, afterwards chatting, and then finally pensively looking out across the sea.

It was a bright afternoon, on the fourth day of the voyage. The blue sky above, completely cloudless, got everywhere into the even bluer sea. Distantly across the water, we occasionally saw the Egyptian coast, shining in the sunlight – a hazy white strip on the horizon. As we got closer, little by little the nearer shore came into focus, and one after another the details of the landscape became visible. There were a group of palms in a gap in the white strip, and miscellaneous shaped shadows these showing to be constructions and villages.

While we, with anticipation, continued to watch the emerging vision to which we travelled, a dim point separated itself from the panorama and approached us. A more careful examination showed it to be a tug, and it stopped next to us; a ladder was thrown down and several brightly dressed and turbaned shapes, together with various dark men in European dress, came on aboard the ship. Arrogantly and without respect they went to the captain's cabin, where they were received as respected individuals, because they are customs officials.

In the meantime, our fishy guardians having already gone away, the two escort vessels went ahead in order to look for any hazards. Soon they signalled to us that there were no hazards and we went ahead to the harbour remarkably easily because of the large lighthouse at the end of the jetty.

After an hour of skilful piloting, the ship's captain took the ship across the outer harbour, where an amazing mixture of shipping was tied up in picturesque confusion; there were native "dhows" and small coastal commercial steamships, each of them important in their own way, as were the many luxurious ocean liners and many modern naval vessels, with which they "confronted the maritime felons". Finally we reached the inner quay where our good ship finished its last but one voyage, carrying into the mysterious east many curious and wondering people.

(In it's following voyage the ship "Aragon" was sunk, hit by a German torpedo.)

Soon the preparations for disembarkation began. The men gathered at the sides of the ship, eagerly looking at the new sights. The guns and previously packed equipment had been stood on the decks; probably in those places, where they would most likely trip up the inattentive. Some men were still very busy packing their possessions in the very small carriers. Here and there groups of soldiers played the last card game, as though coming to the new land is an everyday business, at the same time sitting on the possessions of others who were frantically looking for them. Others played the very popular soldiers game – which is – to evade the corporals who attempted to organize working parties.

A collection of those easy-going souls, who always refuse to be troubled or hurried, together with those who were already prepared, gathered at the landward side of the ship and attempted to get a first sight of the shore. Another group leant over at the other side of the ship in order to buy nuts, fruits and many other kinds of things from the natives, whose oriental miscellanies were defiantly sold without permission, from the boats below. From time to time, a police

86

boat would come and the vendors, who were able, rapidly left in order to avoid baton beatings. One amusing sight I saw there, was when the cooks somewhere in the middle part of the ship poured out large quantities of dirty water and cooking remnants. Unfortunately directly below the place of ejection it landed on the boat in which sat a brightly dressed vendor, who was suddenly covered by this filth. What a surprise for him. How much he became angry and shouted, at the same time gesticulating with his hands, and how the soldiers laughed!!!

Even the most unimaginative traveller would sense some astonishing curiosity on entering an oriental harbour, because of the new sights and strange people, to whom one had already been introduced through the history and traditions known to everyone. Before going ashore, I had thought a lot about the question of what the modern Egyptians will be like. Soon I went to the other side of the ship in order to look at the quay. Immediately below me was the quay, looking very like any quay at home. There were railway tracks, and behind were the usual unpleasant goods and sheds. Because it was intended that we had to disembark, the movement of many goods had already begun. The portage of the battalion was being disembarked and put into large heaps in a convenient place for loading into trucks. Here in the middle of this scene occurred loud altercations between the locals.

Some of the disorderly, ill-dressed humanity of every age and height were apparently occupied carrying our properties from the ship's side to the depository near the wagon. This crowd was dressed in an unusual diversity of torn clothing, generally a dirty white, but some red or blue. The feet of these porters were shoeless. One began to think, that because of the hoarseness of the voices now loud in the flow of malediction and insults, that this strange looking people weren't women (that being assumed from the form of the clothes) but men. In fact, for the foreigner, the voice is the only means of being able to recognise the difference between the sexes. One of the porters, very tall, gaunt and bent under the heavy load, on suddenly meeting a small fat black person, immediately threw off his load and began an angry, wordy quarrel with him. They shouted one against the other for some time, furiously gesturing. Meanwhile other porters sat very relaxed on the ground. The argument rapidly and became more heated. Each became menacingly, as if he is ready to capture and grasp the throat of his opponent. All of a sudden an interruption came. A number of painful blows on their backs, rapidly given by a strong British soldier with thick rod.

He was a bystander and noticed that the work had been interrupted and his blows were in a way a sober cure. Without any question or much ado, the two fighters rapidly took their loads and accordingly went on their appropriate journeys. Many of us, seeing this happen, felt sympathy for those beaten. Others laughed, thinking it was an amusing spectacle. Myself, I didn't know what to think, for although I had some sympathy for those beaten, at the same time thought that the man with the thick stick probably understood the situation better. We realised soon after that only by this method it was possible to make them work. They didn't know any other method and any more favourable treatment is abused. Actually it is a punishable crime for a British soldier to beat a native – but in the military legal code, the crime occurs only if some official sees it.

Along with this detachment of native labourers is a small man, apparently of some higher class, who acted as a kind of gang master or "Raj", as he was called. He carried a thick leather whip so he is able to dispense justice among his subordinates. When any sign of idleness or disobedience appeared, he never lost the opportunity to use the privilege of his superior position. This would be what remained of the ancient system of the hiring for work of the gang masters. The labourer, beaten in this way very rarely defended himself, but stole away in the manner of a whipped cur.

"So, behold the modern Egypt", I thought, seeing the sights before me. Understandably these people are from the lowest ranks and probably I will see much better things later. I was without illusions and many of the pictures in my mind about Egypt were at once dispelled.

So by evening the order came to disembark, and at 9 o'clock on the 3rd of July, I had taken my first step onto the land of Egypt and the continent of Africa. We didn't remain on the ground for long because we were immediately entrained to make the journey south to Ismailia, a town on the side of one of the salt lakes through which the Suez Canal goes. The night was moonless and very dark, and because of this we couldn't see the countryside through which we sped. Apart from this, we were very tired and I soon fell asleep despite the uncomfortable seat that I had in a corner of the wagon. After some sleep, the stopping of the train and the noise of the native voices woke me. I found that we had reached a station called Zag-a-Zig. Loudly shouted the various vendors, who were selling eggs, trinkets and much else. I myself bought some eggs, that were cheap enough. But because I really didn't know the value of Egyptian money and because the Egyptian worker and vendors are almost all robbers, I didn't get value. Fortunately from the Egyptian's point of view, I didn't to begin to learn this until sometime later. Several vendors sold "whisky" and "wine" which many of the soldiers bought. Later when the train had restarted its journey, they began to drink their purchases and found that it was only water and – even very unpleasant – not being very pure water. So the first impressions of the land and its occupants weren't very favourable, and I at once knew that one must take a very cautious approach to these crafty people. My purchases weren't too bad. The eggs were well cooked and as hard as leather; but I was young and hungry and enjoyed eating them well enough. Later I discovered that the Egyptians didn't cook the eggs by boiling in water but in the sand. The very hot sun shining on them, shallowly buried in the sand, soon cooks them in the same way as the heating with boiling water as one usually cooks them at home.

In the morning, after an eight hour journey, we arrived at Ismailia and detrained near an enormous camp. Tents, tents; so many distant, as far as the eye could see there were tents. In the other direction one could see nothing but sand, which extended to the point on the horizon where the sand dunes met the sky. In the other direction a group of palm trees caught the eye, between which houses were to be found, and there was the outskirts of Ismailia, a fine town on the Suez Canal.

I with my comrades were happy to be able to stretch our legs, and we marched with the regiment to an unoccupied part of the camp which was our home for some time. There we found that tea was prepared for us and that drink was very tasty. After a meal, we were left to sleep, and this I found easy on the soft sand in my tent after the tiring journey. The temperature there was very high, and although we were already accustomed to the warm atmosphere of the Salonika region, it was again necessary that we became acclimatised to this much warmer place. Because of this we passed the time pleasantly. During the daytime we rested in the camp. In the mornings and evenings we undertook military exercises to become accustomed to the new conditions. Marches and manoeuvres across the soft sand hills; practice in making bivouacs from rifles and blankets. Although we carried out exercises only two hours during the evening and morning, I found that the conditions were troublesome and hard going in these first days. From time to time we were allowed to visit the town and I passed a pleasant time exploring my first oriental town.

After some time in wild places, how many young women there were of fine appearance! But they were always with female relatives from the white dignitaries in the town, and they were too proud to speak to ordinary soldiers. Of course there were plenty of native beauties of doubtful moral standard, but none of us wished to risk befriending these beauties. One of the very unpleasant sights of the place was the children of the poor. There they sat in groups near the road. Around them zoomed millions of flies. Not only that, but the flies also rested on their faces. The mouths, the noses, the eyes of all of these children here were covered with swarms of flies and, more than, this the children themselves were not at all bothered by the flies. I had never seen anything like it, and I was very unhappy at the sight. The only interest that these children had was to be beggars. Always when a pedestrian went by they all cried "give it baksheesh Johnny" (Give us money, sir). It was said as a joke about the Egyptian children that they came into the world at their birth with a hand outstretched crying "Baksheesh". On other hand the town with its white walled houses, between the green palms that stood near a blue lake in the middle of golden sands, presented a fine-looking picture. I felt that I could remain here contentedly. One or two days I had the opportunity to swim in the salt water lake, and it was very pleasant. It was a fact that during the two weeks when we remained there, I felt that the soldier's life worth living.

But, on earth, it is not always possible to be in an eternal paradise, and soon the order came to prepare to leave the town in order to go somewhere unknown; it was only known that we had to march for three days. We started the task marching on a good road and between many of the towns we went ahead easily enough, although we sweated because of the warmth of the rays of the overwhelming sun and the weight of the things that all of us carried on our backs. But image our chagrin and anger when immediately after the last of the towns, the road disappeared into nothing and we could see nothing in front of us but soft sand, the particles of which were more like dust than grains of sand.

The sun, little by little, subsided and we marched forward through a cloud of dust. We march only 13 kilometres but this march remains in my memory as one of the most difficult things which I ever undertook. The canal station El Ferdan was our goal and we reached it an hour after sunset, tired, wet outside with perspiration but very dry inside from thirst. But the regimental cooks had already begun their duties during the march and soon they were distributing the wanted tea. To really appreciate the value of tea it is necessary to be marching under brilliant sun, with a back aching from the weight of equipment, feet burning and tired, the tongue too big for the mouth and the body feeling as if every drop of moisture has been squeezed out. Then after throwing off the load and stretching the limbs while we lay on our backs on the sand, after then it was the time when a mug of tea seems to be God-sent and tastes like nectar. After a cigarette, and maybe another while we chatted, and soon, one after another the members of the regiment went to sleep there where they were, even without building bivouacs. Only those unfortunates who were on guard duty remained awake.

91

Tranquilly about a thousand men slept deeply under the star-filled oriental sky.

Soon after daybreak, on the 18th of July 1917, the sound of the bagpipes woke us and we got up from our desert beds and prepared to do physical exercises. Afterwards breakfast; and after this we went to the neighbouring canal and swam. The morning was beautiful, the sun rose brilliantly and gave good colours to the distant sand hills; later the air warmed rapidly and a bathe in the canal became extremely enjoyable. The water of the canal had the colour of a delicate emerald green and was surprisingly clear and only slightly salty. This latter property was noticeable after the very salty Lake Timsah near to Ismailia. Swimming easily in this enjoyable water we once again felt as if in paradise. Afterwards we returned to our resting place and built bivouacs in which we passed the very hot midday hours sleeping or reading. In the evening, we once again marched along the dusty road, which went north between the canal and the railway on the right. During this night I saw remarkable sights. While I marched I saw red and green lights to the left. I supposed that it was the signaling system for the canal. But the strange thing was that although we continued to marc forward, the lights always remained on my left hand. I could see nothing else, until suddenly in front of me, I noticed the beams of light on the sand and after several minutes the matter became clear. This was a ship travelling along the canal and from the ship a strong light was directed forward to enable the ship's captain to effectively steer his ship. The small coloured lights that I first saw were on the masts and I saw them first because in that place the banks of the canal were high enough to hide everything apart from the lights on the masts. I couldn't see the masts themselves because of the poor light and at first sight it appeared that the lights floated through the air.

This night we reached another oasis and a station called Tel el Balah. The end of our third march was in Kantara, a large military camp, the largest base in Egypt, and we stayed in the vast area some kilometres from the canal outside the tented area. The reason became evident the next evening, when we marched to the railway station at Kantara

East and boarded a train. This time we travelled unluxuriously in undivided wagons and the journey was one of the most uncomfortable of my whole life. From the look of that wagon, one would suppose that someone had thrown us and our equipment into the wagon, and there we remained in the places where we had landed. We formed one great mixture of arms, legs, bodies, equipment, rifles and sun helmets. Nobody was able to lie down and while the train (more correctly railway train) leaped and shook itself, little by little we settled, but like this we were almost unable to move. If during the night anyone would move themselves in order to find a more comfortable position, he would without fail encounter the face or other part of some comrade and afterwards the night atmosphere would become a reddish blue. I didn't sleep, and because the night was sufficiently light, I was able to see round about. For sometime we were in the heart of a vast desert and I could see nothing except wide sandy places, dressed in a hazy blue light, so very typical of the oriental night, while over head the sky was full of bright stars which seemed to be hanging like innumerable blue lamps.

Another time the route went quite close to the seashore and in the starlight one was able to see the small waves of the Mediterranean gently breaking on the sand. The whole atmosphere was full of charm and mystery and I almost forgot the discomfort of the journey. We went through the night and sometime before dawn we passed close to groups of palms which came more and more often and thicker and finally we stopped in El Arish. Here there was a large hospital and convalescence homes for soldiers and one or two places of amusement. In fact it was a much smaller brother of Kantara. The train remained here for ninety minutes and I went for a swim in the sea with several comrades. The journey continued until 10 o'clock when we reached Dier el Belah (named by the soldiers simply Belah). When we got off the train a strong wind began to blow across the sand and soon we were in the centre of a sand storm, which after our sleepless night and weariness up to that time, troubled us greatly. From a sudden beginning and a sudden end, the cloud of sand moved away eastwards across the desert. We were told that our dwelling place is just next to the sea, and we started to march there. Only three kilometres! But the sand was so very soft that with every step my feet went under until the sand reached my calves. And overhead the sun already high shone hot and compassionlessly on us. It is a miracle that we reached the sea, totally exhausted and only wanting to lie down; but we had to build bivouacs in order to protect ourselves against the brutal rays of the sun. I suppose that in some hours one could see gradual movement into this camp. The name of this place, where we found ourselves, was Shabasi. Here the seashore was somewhat steeper than usual and for this reason the sea threw itself on the sand very strongly. In fact, so strong that it was dangerous to bathe if one was not a strong swimmer. In our regiment were a large number who were and because of this passed a pleasant time during the daily bathe. We remained there eight days and undertook the customary military exercises which the regiment always does during "rests". The soldier always says that he works harder during regimental rest periods than during time on duty. For the first time since our arrival in Egypt we really needed our bivouacs for us to shelter through the night. Until now the only use for the bivouac was to shelter from the heat of the sun, but here next to the sea the nights became colder and because of this heavy dew fell each night, supposedly because of the proximity of the sea. This dew also rusted the metal parts of our rifles which we had to use in order to erect sections of our bivouacs, similar to those which we used in Macedonia, and again we weren't afraid of the dew. The most unpleasant part of erecting a bivouac was the sand which, neither good nor firm, had to hold the pegs to which one tied the strings that held the bivouac upright. Near Belah was a camp for prisoners. It isn't right to call it a camp as there wasn't even one tent for the captive men, but it was only a place enclosed with barbed wire. During the day there wasn't shelter from the sun's rays and compassionate people had hung pieces of material on the wire in order to make a little shade in which they would be able to lay their head. They were a very mixed group of humanity. The Turkish cavalry were lodged apart from the infantrymen as it was considered that cavalrymen were superior to the infantrymen. Those who were deserters from the Turkish army were held in another place and not with the prisoners. In another cage, apart from the Turks, were a number of Bedouin. These were severe-looking warlike men, although the features of several were undoubtedly fine and very dignified. They were captured either as spies for the Turks or in suspicious circumstances in British camps. One older person was a pastor and from time to time he took out a small copy of the Koran from the mysterious folds of his robe, and read out loud from certain excerpts to the lounging gathering. I doubt whether anyone gained any benefit from this, because probably no one paid attention to him and one might suppose that all of them were asleep, except for the fact that if any English soldier should go into the cage every one of those vigilant would get up. In the other cage there stood the only tent in the "camp" and in this was an old woman with a tiny child, whose voice was definitely much too large in proportion to its body. The child cried almost incessantly during the whole night and bothered, not only the soldiers, who guarded the cage, but also the old one who some morning wished to sell it to some soldier for five piaster (of value about one English shilling).

One Sunday evening during the time we remained near Belah, a voluntary religious service was arranged. As requested by the pastor, it was permitted that we could be there without dress uniform, but in any casual clothing. We had just returned from swimming in the sea and most of us wore only a shirt and shorts. Because of the absence of the usual need to wear dress uniform, many soldiers were there. Usually a soldier wouldn't voluntarily go to church parades always because of the inconvenience of dress uniform, but undoubtedly the pastor very pleased to see this good response to the invitation to come to worship God. And I doubt whether similar church services could be more impressive. Imagine five hundred healthy looking men, sitting on the sand in a large double circle, reclining in a variety of positions, the faces tanned from the sun, everyone attentively listening to a tall athletic human being who is silhouetted against the horizon where the magnificent redness of the sky merged with the blueness of the Mediterranean Sea. Indeed it contrasted with the insincerity of some of our modern prejudices. Behold in the pulpit of Christ himself, the free air under a beautiful sky, the Gospel was preached in the self-same land where it had its foundation. This simple ceremony indeed completely represented such an image, which one was visualising of the time when Jesus himself spoke to his countrymen in similar surroundings. Except for the military uniforms, and the exploding shells far away in the direction of the Gaza, the sights and occasion were absolutely peaceful.

The Desert

(Note: The following description of the desert is a transcription from chapter V of "Kilts across the Jordan" by Benard Blaser, whose book greatly helps my recalling the experiences of my visit to the "Near East).

"The desert, the grassless sandy place in which we then found ourselves, wasn't without its own beauties and attractions. Seen in some certain conditions and circumstances, it could present to the sensitive eye some grandeur, which one doesn't often see in other places. Few people wouldn't be impressed by the intense loneliness of the desert its sunsets when the sand so very white and blinding under the daytime sunlight, little after little becomes a dull ochre, being coloured the red by the sun whilst it rapidly and almost visibly disappearing behind the horizon.

The author of "Rothen" says laughingly about the desert: "the ground is so much the same at all times that owns eyes search the sky. One looks for the sun because he is the taskmaster, and according to him one become aware which work remains to be done. He comes when one dismantles the tent in the early morning, and after the first hour he stands at our side and thus informs us that all the day's work remains to be done. Afterwards, for some time, yes a long time, one no more sees him, for one is veiled and hidden and one is afraid to look the strength of his glory. But one knows where he walks supreme because of the touch of his brilliant rays. But the conquering time is always marching forward, and gradually the descending sun is crossing the sky and now tiny touches the other arm, and throws long shadows of the journey on the sand in the direction of distant Persia."

This kind of charm is the legend and mystery of the desert. This enables one to easily contemplate romantic images, when this grandiose solitude extends endlessly onwards!! This solitude in which dwells unnamed secret loves and adventures, uneasiness and death, which one will never able to completely uncover.

Even the bones, which lay here and there whitened by the sun, fill the air with a tragic mystery, and suggests a perpetual tale about dissatisfaction from suffering. See there the disintegrating bones of some unfortunate human, and there standing out of the sand, the remains of a faithful animal. Who was the unfortunate one and what were the circumstances in which he met death, no one will ever know. But, there is the evidence, smooth and white unnamed and unidentifiable; and there it stays until the time when the elements who destroyed them finally engulf them.

We were coming to know the desert. It will be our home for a long unknown time. Every one of its diverse aspects and features, its beauty and its uncompassionate cruelty will soon become well know to us. Picturesque caravans are not coming beautifully to our 'sight'; we will no more be seeing forms rolled up in coloured robes sitting on camels, which unenergetically and mechanically badly walked, one after another across the sand. No, for us will be the hash difficult realities of wartime, with every combination of terrors and interchanging successes and failures.

Sitting in a tent near Ismailia on the evening of the 7th of July 1917, I worked in order to send a letter to my father.

Dear Dad,
        I understand that you asked me why I wasn't writing home for almost two weeks. The reason is that we were moved away from Greece, and now continuing our journeys around the world. We find ourselves in Egypt, and my address now is -----. We left our position in the battle line in Greece when another regiment replaced us and after two days started to march to Salonika. This marching was wholly agreeable because of the fact that we marched by night and rested by day. One day we rested by a river and

enjoyed a good swim. The most unpleasant night was the last, when we marched passed the place where our camp was when we reached Salonia six months before. Understandably, that night when we came to that place, we thought that we were reaching the end of the march, but we had to march two or three kilometres more. When we finally halted, we found that the ground is so hard, that some iron and almost all the wooden nails, which we usually used for fixing our bivouacs, broke. Finally we used our bayonets as "wooden nails" and the rifles as tent poles. When we laid in the bivouacs we found that the gun sights work well as candle holders. Ho, what would the adjutant have said if he were to see that. He would probably go mad!

During the two or three days which followed, we practiced an attack against an imaginary enemy on the plain. The grand finale was an attack during which we had live cartridges in our machine guns. A stack of biscuit tins had been set up in front to represent the enemy and after the end of the attack none of the biscuit tins was capable of holding even a drop of water.

The most remarkable thing in this camp was the visit of the Bulgarian aeroplanes. If the arrival of an enemy aeroplane was noticed, the camp was warned and when we heard the alarm we had to run from the camp to disperse and hide ourselves as far away as possible. If the Bulgarian came while we were parading or doing military exercises we thought that this is a good joke – but if he came when we were free then we whole heartedly cursed his peevishness.

After one week while being alive to the most extraordinary rumours, we collected our properties and marched to the dock, where we were hurried onto a ship without delay. From the ship I enjoyed the most pleasant view of the town of Salonika. During our stay in this part of the world I never received permission to visit the town myself.

I am sending to you one or two mementoes and I hope that these arrive safely in London. Please inform me whether or not you received them.

*Our voyage was agreeable. As usual my section had
to set up the machine gun against possible submarine attack.
Our place was on the highest deck, in the middle of the left
side of the ship. We were able to guess that our section was
important – on land we are anti-aircraft and on the sea we
were antisubmarine defence. However we were a happy
little family who gained the most possible pleasure from the
life, which was given to us. Two new machine guns were
given to our company and a section was proposed but we
preferred to remain together in the "family".*

*During the voyage the weather was very good and
the sea calm, and although the ship wasn't as comfortable as
that in which we travelled to Salonika, I greatly enjoyed it.
When we stopped against the quay at the end of the voyage,
we saw a very interesting panorama. Groups of natives
unloaded the ship. We threw cigarettes and coins to children
on the quay and the attempts of the dock policemen to chase
away the urchins was an amusing sight. He chased one
group menacingly with a large stick and while he chased
one group away another came from the other direction.*

*Soon we disembarked and travelled by train into the desert.
We reached our destination the following morning and there
we couldn't see anything other than sand which stretched
everywhere so far as one was able to see.*

Sights of Egyptian Things

We were lodged in a camp of large army tents and it was a pleasure to have a dwelling into which we were able to walk instead of crawling in on one's stomach, as we had to do in order to enter our own self made bivouacs.

The evening after our arrival, we bathed ourselves in a very salty lake and this was very good. In our "family" are three or four good swimmers and we swam enough distance from the shore as far as the shallower part of the lake where the sand came up almost as far as the level of the water. The water was the saltiest that I had ever tasted and if one accidentally drank any -- well then --.! However the swim was so very refreshing in that burning land, that we all always longed for the arrival of the hour for our visit to the lake.

Today I am going into a neighbouring town to make a visit in order to see what an Egyptian town is like and supposedly have my photograph taken in my eastern clothes. [sf - p.130]

One day, before than we quit Greece, we lived through a sand storm. The air was full of sand just like a dense cloud carried by the wind. We had to hold firmly our bivouacs and all the loose things so that they didn't fly away. Several of my comrades were asleep when the storm started and before they woke, their bivouacs, blankets, papers, etc, escaped or flew into the sea. Just after the end of the sand storm a rain storm came and those things which had not been blown away were now nearly flooded. I quickly undressed myself and went outside in order to dig a channel around the tent and in this way saved our home from death by drowning. But in fact the rain was welcome for it wiped the body clean of the dust which had got in everywhere. Speaking more of my own Greek memories of the beautiful views which we saw from our various positions in the battle front. Everywhere the view was similar, as below!

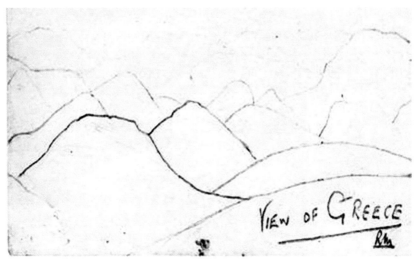

View of Greece

So I must now finish. Hoping that this letter will find you well and will soon be sending a letter to
                    Your loving son
                        Robin."

One must note that in the above letter I didn't mention the names of the various places that we passed through. It was because of an order, that nothing in a letter should to say anything which could possibly be useful information to the enemy, if he should capture the letters, or if a spy should pass on any information included in a letter. Often the dispatch of letters was totally forbidden, and always an officer of the company had to read through each letter in order to delete the forbidden information. When letters were not allowed, postcards were distributed on which were diverse phrases from which the soldiers could chose the most suitable for informing their families about themselves.

Here are details:-

1. <u>Address-side</u>

  King Battle Camp   Sign   Service
  Now write
        The address on this side
        If anything else is added the card will be destroyed

The card doesn't need a postage stamp. The post official stamp every card with an impression with the words (Field Post Office) "Battle Camp Post Office", the date and the number of the brigade.

2. Other side

Nothing should be written on this side except the date and the signature of the sender. Strike out those phrases which don't apply. If anything else is written, the card will be destroyed.

> I am quite well.
>
> I am now in hospital
>> (sick) and making good progress.
>> (wounded) and hope to leave here soon.
>
> I'm being sent to the base.
>>> (letter from ....
> I am in receipt of your (telegram from ....
>>> (package from ....
> A letter is following as soon as possible
> I have not received a letter from you   (last time
>>>> (for a long time
>
>> Now signature)   Robin
>>> date   20.7.17

(a postal cost must be paid relative to the letter or postcard addressed to sender of these postcards.)

By means of red ink I am showing the manner in which I used this kind of card, which I sent to my brother on the 20th July, when we were in camp near the Suez Canal at Kantara.

Our stay near the sea ended on the 29th of July and although we didn't know it then, we said goodbye to the lovely sight of the sea, not to seen again for a long time. In the afternoon we paraded ready to go away somewhere as ordered. We didn't know our objective but a place in the desert was spoken about. The whole battalion gathered in a large oasis of palms, surrounded by cactus hedges. In this oasis was an ancient well of stone, constructed it is said in the year 920. We filled our water bottles with delicious cold water, from under a platform made by comrades of other regiments.

At the appointed hour the brigade began to march, my regiment at the end of the corps. We crossed the railway and continued the journey across a hill. Almost all the ground was soft and we found ourselves on dusty sand. It wasn't good sand but unpleasant dirty grey dust which rose up in the air when one put a foot on the ground. Soon the first regiments of the brigade were lost from sight in a dense cloud. One is able to imagine the state of those unfortunates who marched in the rear sections of the corps. One was unable to see, one breathed in the sand with every breathe. One perspired and the dust went into the streams of sweat which flowed down our bodies. At first we laughed at the comic sight of our mates, but not long after we weren't capable of joking; we now felt the weight of our loads and felt suffocated because of the sand in the air. It was the custom for us to march for fifty minutes – one couldn't say "march" but "foot dragging" for on that ground one was not able to march – and finally the welcome signal came for the hourly halt. The pleasure that we felt in that moment must be experienced to be believed. However suffice to say that the removal of our equipment and laying it out on the ground took only a few seconds. The halt lasted only ten minutes and we greatly wished not to lose even one minute of that beneficial rest. Now the ten minutes passed too quickly, and the order came for the recommencement of the going forward. And in this manner we toiled during the journey. After three hours the dust cloud became so dense, that a two hour halt was ordered – a situation very, very unusual in my soldier's life. We were allowed to wash our mouths with water from our water bottles, but were strongly forbidden to drink any.

We lay there for the whole period, too weary to move, almost too exhausted for talking, until finally again the order came to begin the march. And we continued suffering until the end of the journey to Sheikh Nuran, which was found to be almost 20 kilometres away from Deir el Belah. From time to time we passed a man, of another regiment, lying near the road, too weak to continue the attempt. Our regiment has a strong tradition that no one would leave the march; so to maintain this tradition, the comrades of any unfortunate individual incapable of carrying his load, everyone helped him so that he would not besmirch the regimental tradition about abandoning the march. My regiment was very proud that day, for in the brigade only we didn't lose one man during the march.

The following day we left Sheikh Nuran and continued our struggle against the desert sand. After some time we met motor roads which were very much better than the rotten roads like those we had marched on the previous day. Those motor roads were built for the ambulances, which transported the sick and wounded from the battle line to the armies battle camp hospital some way behind the position. The surface of the road was made by removing the upper layer of the sand until the firm ground was reached. That valiant work was done by the Egyptian workers which the army had employed in order to construct the road and to remove any sand blown onto it. When night fell we saw lamplights in the gloom which announced to us that we had reached our objective. Soon we entered a little valley surrounded by some tiny sand hills. After some time the first marchers reached a large white strip which lay across from our road. At once a loud scratching sound was hear, which was very noticeable after the previous silence. A regiment, marching by night is not normally silent. From time to time one hears the sound of the taps of the handle of the trenching tool against other parts of the equipment swinging against the body, cause by the marching. In these circumstances the column appears like a snake, which is creeping forward across the sand.

That large white strip mentioned, which appears very white in the bright moonlight, is the river bed of the Wady Ghuzzah (pronounced U Gazi). Because of the dry summer weather there remained no water; only the large white stones over which the water flows in the rainy season. The Wady (means small river valley), moreover was not very wide, between ten and a hundred yards, although up to a distance as much one thousand metres away one found hillocks and river beds formed by the winter floods. Beyond the more distant hills was the front line of the British soldiers. We marched between the hillocks to the other side of the wady.

My company continued the march as far as the trenches, where we found a company of the 1/4 Welsh Regiment, one of the regiments of the 53a Division, whose replacements we were. We formally occupied the positions, and the Welshmen marched way. Before us the desert laid silent and peaceful, one couldn't have imaged that we were already in the battle line.

That point in the Wady Ghuzzeh was called Shellal, although nothing at all exists, dwelling or other construction or place, which would have given the place a right to have a name. The little valley lay at the end of the sandy desert of Sinai.

The battle line was a simple matter. A system of defensive places was constructed, with one every 500 yards. One platoon guarded every defence position. By day those on duty (in every defence position) consisted of one non-commissioned officer and five soldiers, but by night the whole platoon stood guard, divided into five or six groups inclusive of the listening group, who were located at the entrance through the barbed wire. The deeper small valley to the rear gave a hiding place for a whole army, although if it were observed from a modern aeroplane, the place would be much less concealed.

In that place there, like everywhere we found ourselves after arrival in Egypt, it was terribly warm during the day. To go into the open air without a sun helmet between 11 o'clock and 3 o'clock in the afternoon was a punishable crime. Because of that heat, and because of the hundreds of flies, sleeping in the daytime was almost impossible. For even a little sleep, we found that it was necessary to completely cover the bare parts of the body. We had already been given pieces of anti-mosquito netting, but that was only sufficient to cover the face, and one had to use other objects in order to cover the other parts. And these additional covers only increased the heat and were no help in getting any sleep.

Our general position was at the right flank of the line, and in order to defend us and further prevent the enemy's ability to bypass us away into the desert, it was arranged that a strong group of cavalry would be on duty there to the front and to the side of us. These cavalry groups were either Australian detachments or English county regiments. The left flank of the Turks stretched to Beersheba, 15 miles away (24 kilometres). Going eastward, the two lines became closer, until near Gaza, the two armies were close enough for proper trench warfare

The landscape in front of Shellal was a barren wilderness, sparsely covered with dry grass with infrequent clusters of shrubs. The general effect was very miserable. Those uninteresting vistas enormously increased the monotony of the daytime duty. For two hours one had to stand at one's post without any protection against the very hot sun's rays, except from that given by one's sun helmet. The only duty was to closely watch across that lifeless plain. Mostly the thoughts wandered over every topic except those which related to the Turks or warfare.

And, meanwhile, the imagination begins to play tricks. A small group of trees appear to the right; these are growing on the edge of a pool, on whose surface the rays of the bright sun are shining and reflecting; the whole thing simmering in the hot atmosphere. One wondered why one had not noticed this beautiful thing before; but with hind-sight it became clear, that this was only a mirage, a delusion. Then one understands, how in that way the traveller is often deceived when travelling across these places – often until death!

The gaze wanders more to the left. There, to the front, across the flat land, through the haze, a range of low hills was visible. These small hills are really not very far from Beersheba – probably between them the actual Turkish positions were to be found. How many people are defending them? Will we meet them sometime? Will we be going to them, or will they be coming to us first. Is it possible we will go beyond those mountains? And from this reverie, the attention was awakened because of a dust cloud that is appearing. Happily welcoming any change in the life, one attentively watches while the small cloud becomes a cloud, in which one was later able to distinguish the forms of cavalrymen. Who are they? Two; no more; five or only one? Because of the dust it is difficult to decide. After some time, one can clearly see that the group consists of three. They come forward, straight to the entrance through the defence wire. They ride in line, gently trotting, as if on horses tired from a long run. The middle one has clothes different from those of his companions. As the riders came closer, one sees that two strong Australians are coming with a captive. They pass through the wire and dismount. A non-commissioned officer comes forward and receives the Turkish prisoner, whom he sends with two soldiers to the commander of the regiment. The capturers again remount and gallop off in order to find their comrades.

These kinds of occurrence were frequent, several times the prisoners were Turkish cavalrymen who were surprised by our cavalrymen, but sometimes they were deserting infantrymen. By night, it was very worthwhile to watch the cavalry regiments going out on the plains. And we, who must remain in the defence system in order to do extremely uninteresting duties, really envied those romantic people who go out in order to find adventure.

There follows three of the letters which I sent home during our stay there in the line.

30.7.17

Dear Annie,
Here I am again. I am sending a short letter in order to tell you that everything here is going well at present. But one thing I don't understand is that that I haven't received any letter from home. I have received two newspapers but no letter during these past weeks. The post arriving with letters from the home land is one of the most liked things amongst us. I really wish that one of you would be able to write a letter every week. I am sending to you once a week when this is permitted.

How are you all doing? Well I hope. Is Dad very busy now, or is he able to do much work in the potato-patch. I suppose that at present you are growing nothing except vegetables. Greet David and Edie and tell them that I will be waiting for their letters very soon.

After my last letter nothing very significant has happened. While we were in our last camp, we are near the sea and swam twice every day. One wasn't able to do much swimming because of the great strength and very large size of the waves. However, we greatly amused ourselves. We did many military exercises and everything went well. After some time we marched to another place. This march was across the desert. Here marching was very difficult, because all the times it was across soft sand. The sand was blown everywhere and the air became full of sand, and one had to breathe it in and swallow it. At the same time it found its way into the eyes. The sooner we will be able leave this place the better it will please me. Now while I am writing a strong wind blows the dust into the air. The dust gets in everywhere and the place is uncomfortable.

I am sending several coins for David. The word AEPTA on the coin is the Greek writing for a mite. The coins with the number 5 are worth a half penny, those with 10 are worth a penny and those with 20 are equivalent to two pennies.

Let me know as soon as possible about their arrival – that is if they reach you.

With love from your dear brother
Robin
P.S.   Please forward the enclosed letters. Those for Mrs Bomford and John Baker need penny postage stamps; you can give Mrs Shrimpton hers.
Love Robin

Dear Annie

It's me again! I am happy to be able to say that I am still enjoying good health.

Thank Dad for the papers which I received not long ago. I had received some letters from before the beginning of July and I have become somewhat disturbed and wish to know how you are. I have read about the air attacks on London, and the probability of bombs being dropped in my part of the city. And because of the absence of a letter I ask myself whether bad things have happened to you. So, please send me letters often. I like them very much, because these letters from home are one of our occasional pleasures.

Since my last letter, nothing of importance or interest has happened. We are still in the same place and participating in every kind of exercise. When we are not on duty in the line our usual daily routine is as this. We get out of bed at 4 o'clock in the morning and do exercises between 4.45 and 5.15. After that, we have breakfast. A parade follows at 6.30. Before this, we must have taken down our bivouacs and cleaned and tidied the place; washed, shaved and cleaned our rifles. Work during this parade usually consists of bayonet practice, dummy attacks, etc, and continue until 9.30. Afterwards we are free to do anything one pleases until five in the evening, because in between these times it gets too hot for work. From time to time, in those free hours an order comes to pack and to be prepared to move off. That is so that we learn to act well, should a real alarm occur. Several times it was said that those interruptions from our afternoon rests will happen because the colonel is not able to sleep and in an unfriendly way thinks that some others are able to rest then. After the dinner at 4.30, we pass more than an hour or even two exercising.

In the machine gun section we avoid the morning parade because of the need to clean our gun. And today we did our turn as anti-aircraft defenders. Two or three days before we had been able to fire the gun. I did well enough.

The largest part of our transport animals here are camels. They are strange animals. When one puts loads on the camel that animal has to kneel. When camels do that they look as if they are folding themselves. It is a very amusing business. The guides are usually light brown Egyptians. These people sing in a psalm-chanting manner while they march. The same, not very long, phrase repeating it many times, like a refrain. The whole business is very monotonic and unmusical. Sometimes, one of them sings verses continuously in a very high voice.

Everyone from our section is doing well. Our corporal, Bill Finlay, is now in Cairo in order to learn something about the Vickers machine gun. He is having a very good time there.

This is the end of the news from here.
How are you in Belmont Villa
Don't forget to write to me soon!
With much love from your brother
Robin

P.S. Nowadays we really have to sign our letters.
R. Murray

Afterwards I am writing as follows to my brother:-

Dear David,
I am not going to write you a long letter, but only a note to say something about the coins which am enclosing. The Egyptian basic coinage is one piastro and is worth two and a half pence. The large coin, in which there is a hole, is a one piastro. At one side of the hole is a number "10", and at the other the sign ١٠. *The* ١٠ *is the Egyptian writing for 10. I will show you the Arabian symbols which one uses here.*

English	1	2	3	4	5	6	7	8	9	0
	١	٢	٣	٤	٥	٦	٧	٨	٩	٠

On the other side of the coin you will notice the date in Arabic. The Arabs don't calculate the date from the birth of Christ, but from the birth of Mahomet, and so that their date isn't the same as the English. So you will see that their date for 1917 is ١٣٣٥, which (you can notice from the above table) equals 1335.

On the small coin which is two piastro (1¼ pence) the actual Arab date represents 1916. This is because of the fact that their year doesn't start in January like ours. The two coins are without a doubt old Egyptian piastros. The dates on these are ١٣٢٧ (1327) and ١٢٩٣ (1293). The copper coin is an Argentinean penny.

I can't write anymore. Because the canteen is being opened and I want to go there to buy several things, mainly food.

Love to you all, from your brother,
Robin

From time to time, we had among us groups of Egyptian and Arab workers – members of the Egyptian Labour Corps. They cared for and led the camels, which were used to carry water containers and other necessary military things. They were very bad workers and all the time the supervisor must always be vigilant to ensure that those workers did their jobs. One method of making them work was through singing. They sang some tunes monotonically, at the same time working to the rhythm. Often, from amongst them was one man who acts as a soloist and conductor. I don't know whether these soloists sang according to known written words; because the long duration of the singing, I believe that the soloist made up the words while they sang. Often they became very excited and danced and gestured and warmed and excited their singing comrades. The soloist generally sang in a very high pitch while the others sang the refrain lower. The music wasn't very pleasing to the western ear, but apparently the labourers really enjoyed it and without doubt worked much better while they sang.

After the war I met a good-hearted Esperantist, who had soldiered in Egypt and Palestine. He has on many occasions studied these workers and he learnt the words of several from these refrains. These he has sent to me in a letter, and as they would be of interest to you, I will enclose here excerpts from afore mentioned letter.

"At present I am enclosing several examples of the songs we heard in Egypt, but it isn't possible for me to translate them completely.

The first deals with a very brave man and his fiancée.

Tuli ani a-wel, Tuli a----~~~hi Gawa el waha beebi wali ga----hi

I don't understand the second at all, only recognising it because of frequent repetition.

Jum-jilla sari ra buĝa libla dah ba'ejn

The third air is one of the most frequently heard, and has two singing themes; (a) translated "How many nights, how many days" (until we return to ----), (b) is a love song where the words mean "so, my fiancée! I greet you"   Here is the music and Arabic words.

✗ Vidu la noton ✗ sur paĝo 112

(a) Kam lej-lo, kam yom
(b) Ja ha bee-bi salaamat

The pronunciation of this "ra" is a throat sound as in French.

The comma shows sounds which cannot be depicted, but I'm not bothering you with this, because many people cannot even make the sound.

The fourth is a song which the Alexandrians sing about their city.

Skandaria is the Arabic name for Alexandria.

Because I was not a skilled musician this was not easy for me to show to you the delightful music notes but I have tried to do what I can.

Notwithstanding, this I think you will easily recognise the airs if you play according to the notes on the piano.

This was the way my Esperanto friend wrote. The third I easily recognise immediately, only seeing the notes and words, which I recognised, because they were the most popular and most often sung between the workers. The others sounded vaguely familiar to my ears. Possibly after some years I have forgotten the ones not heard often.

We stayed in this place at Shellal until the 26th of August, when another division came to occupy our position. We went away to a place called El Sho'uth, four miles behind the line. At El Sho'uth, which understandably was in the sandy region, there were some small areas surrounded by hedges of cacti. We called those areas "cacti gardens" although they contained only scrub-like growth and shrubs. And we used this "garden" as our home for some time while we did special exercises in order to become accustomed to living and warfare in the desert.

The living was somewhat disagreeable during the day, because besides the heat and the flies, about which I have already written, we found other torments here. Each day, sometime before noon a warm dry wind began to blow. That almost always continued until sunset. But then an even more unpleasant aspect was the sudden change and brought with it a lot of sand. Often we had just received food when the sudden cloud of sand came to spoil the soup or other foods.

And we also felt the unpleasantness of a great thirst in the absence of water. There we learnt the value of water. Where we dwelt there was no water. It was brought twice a day on camels. Each regiment had about twenty camels which visited la Wady Ghuzzeh twice a day to bring our water from the wells built by the engineers. Officially there was a daily provision of two quarts for each of us, this equals 2.272 litres; one for drinking and one for cooking tea or soup, etc. About washing one said nothing. But we had to shave ourselves, wash ourselves, from time to time clean clothes – and everything using this 'vast' amount of water.

There was one useful interesting thing to be found there at El Sho'uth. That was some numbers of chameleons. We experimented with them in order to discover whether or not they changed their colour to match the surface on which they found themselves. Those experiments were successful enough. But we found that they have a greater useful habit. They really liked flies and we were greatly amused to watch them suddenly shoot out the very long tongue in order to capture an unsuspecting fly. Another curiosity was their ability to move the eyes independently. In this way they were able to look in two directions at the same time. I had one of these friends in my bivouac the whole time when we dwelt in the "cactus garden".

The pattern of life was also unusual for us because of the midday heat, which made us work in the evening, by night and early in the morning and resting during the day. One heard rumours about a forthcoming attack and so more and more we prepared ourselves in order to participate in that matter.

On the 19th of September, 1917, we got out of bed at 4 in the morning and paraded for exercises with our machine gun to 5.30. After the rest in the middle of the day we again paraded at 4 o'clock in the afternoon, loaded the mules and marched cross the sand for four hours as far as Lone Tree Hill, near to the Wady Ghuzzeh where we camped at 8.30 in the evening in order to pass the night.

On the 20th we woke at 5 o'clock in the morning and after breakfast we passed two or three hours exercising with our machine gun and also estimating distances. The latter was very necessary because we were unaccustomed to the clarity of the atmosphere which altered the aspect of the landscape compared with what we found in the lands where we had been before. We rested through the middle of the day and at 5 o'clock we repacked everything and marched home to the "Cactus Garden". During the evening we passed two or three hours near a fire singing until 9 o'clock when we went to bed.

The following day we had a rest time and when, knowing the reason before hand, we marched to the Wadi in the evening. There we met the rest of the brigade that passed the whole night on practice attacks. Those manoeuvres finished at 6.30 and we went back to the starting point for breakfast at 9.30. Afterwards we marched back to our desert home which we reached at noon. The march in the great heat of the middle of the day was extremely tiring. In the evening a big concert was arranged for the whole division; but because of fatigue and the fact that we would have had to march to the place I decided not to go. I remained in my bivouac and went to sleep soon after 8.30.

The following morning I had to parade with several comrades to go with the camels to Shellal in order to bring the water for the regiment. Near the watering place we found some water melons which were very delicious and refreshing because of the amount of juice some of them contained. After our task at Shellal we got back to the camp at 11 o'clock.

There we heard many rumours about moving away in the evening that day. However soldiers learn to be fatalists and we didn't allow ourselves too much unhappiness because of an unpleasant change. Instead we arranged a sing-song in order to cheer ourselves up and the regimental padre, who happened to be passing, stopped and sang with us. At the time we had enough good singers in our section, and soon collected a big crowd of our comrades in order to sing with us.

The members of our section are called:-

Corporal	Finlay	who between ourselves is				"Bill"
Private	Brinson	"	"	"	"	"Berbie"
"	Murray	"	"	"	"	"Bob"
"	Bullock	"	"	"	"	"Johnnie"
"	Marsh	"	"	"	"	"Vi"
"	Clifton	"	"	"	"	"Clif"
"	Golder	"	"	"	"	"Goldie"
"	Dennis	"	"	"	"	"George"

These were a happy little family who, under the leadership of Bill, went through the military life well enough, without trouble. We were proud of our reputation as a section and worked strongly and skilfully together.

The corporal, Bill Finlay, was a tall blond individual with blue eyes. He was a typical Englishman; strong, capable, good hearted and a natural leader of people. We would do anything to please him. Because of this our section was one of the happiest and best in the regiment. Bill readily worked us when necessary, but at the same time, he knew how to play and sing with us when free moments occurred. So, in spite of the occasional unpleasant circumstances, our "family" was able to enjoy, if not an always agreeable soldier's life, one without continual grumbling.

That evening the post from home came and my notebook especially alludes to the arrival of one letter from my sweetheart. But apparently we didn't have much time in order to read our letters, because at 6.30 in the evening we paraded in ordered to march to the firing range near Lone Tree Hill. We began to march at 7.15 and reached our objective at 9 o'clock. After our arrival, we immediately erected our bivouacs and after a welcome cigarette we went to sleep at 9.45.

We woke at 4.30 in the morning and ate at 5 o'clock. Afterwards our section went to the firing range in order to practice the use of our machine gun. Each member of the section must fire about 50 bullets, all the while doing various actions according to the orders of Corporal Bill. When this exercise came to an end we marched back to the camp, and rested while others did their practice. At noon we again went to the firing range. This time we exercised firing with our normal rifles. Back again to the camp in order to find and drink the very good cup of tea and afterwards enjoy some rest. Soon the order came to parade, immediately followed by a counter-order. From time to time more orders and changes came. Finally at 4.30 pm, we again paraded and marched to the firing range in order to take part in more firing practice. That exercise was interrupted because of the arrival of some Australian cavalry who rode across the wady. While they went passed, my thoughts flew across the desert to where the riders were going. I envied them, who were really experiencing a much more interesting life than mine. At least they went to search for the enemy while we had to remain in our desert home parading, exercising, etc. But now they went away and we had to recommence our work. When we had finished everything we marched back to the camp. That evening very good community singing took place between us. Our section was constructing a big bivouac for the family. Here is a picture copied from that made by our artist comrade Clif.

[the picture is no longer available]

The roof consisted of two blankets tied together and tied with cord to a shrub at one end and to a pole at the other end. The cord was fixed to two pegs holding firmly in the ground in order to make the top of the roof rigid. The lower edge of the roof was firmly held by cords and pegs. We dug out the ground under the roof so that we could have access to our sitting place and table. We found that home more comfortable and cooler for living in during daytime. At night we slept either under the starry sky or in pairs in smaller bivouacs.

After our evening meal Bill Finlay suggested singing. We started and soon the others in the camp collected around us and together we sang the favourite melodies from the home land. Understandably not always according to the orthodox words of the original.

Tuesday the 25th of September 1917. Woke at 4.30 in the morning. Ate at 5 o'clock; at 5.30 paraded carrying a machine gun. Marched to the firing range, but there was some mistake and we didn't fire, and we returned into the camp. Paraded at 2 pm and marched to the firing range where we took part in a firing exercise. I returned to the camp at 5 o'clock, leaving the other members of the section to finish their exercise. Because of the late return of the others this evening past very quietly.

Wednesday 26th September. Woke at 5 o'clock. Ate at 6 o'clock. This day was completely without the usual parades and we amused ourselves in the cactus garden – reading, writing and sleeping. At 12.20 we paraded and marched to Shellal near which place the engineers were constructing deeper wells and a very large reservoir order to store water. There we found shower baths with warm water and our old friend the fumigator. So we undressed ourselves, made packages of our clothes after taking out everything of leather, gave the packages to the man in charge of the machine and went in order to bathe ourselves. This finished we sat near the fumigator, dressed only by a sun helmet in order to wait until the "cooking" of our clothes was finished. In fact in Egypt and Palestine, between us, we were not finding so many insect "friends" as in the other lands which we had visited. Supposedly that, because of the great heat, we took off our clothes as often as possible.

In the evening the musicians of the brigade visited our camp and played to us. Certainly a festive day! Thursday the 27th of September. Woken at 4 o'clock. Breakfast at 5 o'clock. Paraded at 5.30. Exercised our methods of attack in and around the Wady, and returned into the cactus garden at 10.30. Our midday tea was provided at 12.30 and one hour later we paraded in order to repeat the exercises which we had already done in the morning. This time we used live cartridges in our rifles and machine guns firing live bullets as if in a real attack. One very amusing incident happened then in our section. The attack consisted of a number of quick but short forward dashes; after which we threw ourselves to the ground and immediately opened fire on the position attacked. Possibly will be better if I will say a few words about our machine gun which is of a type called Lewis. The bullets are carried in circular magazines, each of which contain 47 bullets. Because of a skilfully designed mechanism, the gun fired about 600 bullets per minute, at the same time ejecting the used cartridges through a hole on the right hand side near the trigger. One didn't often fire all the bullets uninterruptedly, but if that had to be done one had to have a new container after every five seconds. The Lewis machine gun was supported by six men. The gunner carried the gun himself called No.1; No.2 carried the spare parts in order to repair the gun if necessary; when the gun was used in battle, the chief duty of No.2 was to lie near No.1, who fires, and to replace the empty magazine by a full one. In order to do this and to observe and help No.1, the No.2 always lies to the left of No.1. Numbers 3 and 4 carried extra magazines which they passed to No.2 as needed and No.5 and 6 looked after the mules with the rest of the magazines and when necessary run forward to No.3 or No.4 carrying fresh supplies of ammunition. Well that is the way it works. But my story refers only to myself who was No. 1, and Bert Golder who acted as No. 2. In the middle of the attack he and I ran forward. I threw myself onto the ground and immediately fired a burst of twenty bullets. Immediately there was an outcry from my companion Bert. Looking at him I found that in the excitement he had laid himself to my right side instead of to the left, and because of this the ejected cases hit him and battered his hat and one or two hit him on the ear. Although he suffered no damage the affair was somewhat painful for him, and a very good lesson relating to the conduct as a good No. 2. When I saw that Bert was not damaged I laughed a great deal but he didn't like the joke very much.

The practice attack continued and we had a lot of pleasure because of the very good performance of our machine gun. We finished the exercise and found ourselves again in the camp at 5.30 p.m. By evening new rumours came about forthcoming movements away somewhere; everyone or almost everyone of these was the opposite of the previous one and finally we believed none of them.

But on Friday the 28th, we were got out of bed at 4 o'clock, we had breakfast at 5 o'clock, paraded at six, when everything the regiment possessed was already packed on wagons, mules or camels. At 6.30 a.m., we began marching and went a distance of approximately seven miles (11.26 kilometres), north by northeast in three and a half hours. When one remembers that on a good road we will be able march at the rate of more than three miles per hour without trouble, one must take into account the difficulties of desert marching, which slowed us to a rate of two miles per hour, at the same time sweating heavily. At the end of this march we unloaded our animals, set up our bivouacs and at 10.30 had already begun to rest. After a cup of tea we were paraded again at 2 o'clock p.m. and went to enjoy a bathe. In our new desert camp we passed a quiet evening.

The following day (Sunday the 29th of September) we woke up at 4 o'clock in the morning, ate at 5 o'clock, and paraded at 5.30 in order to practice methods of attack. We enjoyed the usual rest between 10 in the morning and 2.30 p.m., when we again made practice attacks. We again reached the camp in the cactus garden at 5 o'clock, where I passed the time reading newspapers from the home land. The canteen had received a quantity of food for sale, and our section decided to arrange a special party meal. Vi Marsh cooked some delicious cocoa on our cook's fire. Tinned fruits, cream and other foods made a luxurious feast for after a long period of simple army nourishment.

Speaking about nourishment, reminds me about one matter which pleased us when we first began living in the cactus garden. That is the so called "prickly pear", the fruit of several of the cacti which formed the hedge or fence, which formed the means of protection for our "cactus garden". The prickly pear (from the Latin - opuntia engelmanni) is a species of cactus whose trunk and leaves are flat. The leaves grow not only from the trunk but also from other leaves in a very amusing strange manner. On the leaves and on the underside of the leaves are many cruel thorns in order to dissuade the thirsty people who are trying to reach the fruit. The flowers of these plants are yellow or reddish, and the fruit are red and similar to the shape of a pear. The fruit was covered with a black fluff which effectively was thousands of very unpleasant thorns which were very troublesome to anyone whose hand was pierced. The edible part of the fruit was somewhat sweet flavour, very juicy and refreshing. In order to get one of those fruit one must hit it with a stick in order to make it fall from the plant; with a fork or something similar, one must hold it while one cuts away the shell with the thorny down; and then the desirable and delicious fruit remains ready for eating. Several men who first found these fruit and didn't know about the unpleasantness, many cursed because of the pain in the hands and especially in the lips and mouth.

On Sunday the 30th of September, we weren't allowed to enjoy our usual rest and church service, but we had to go in order to do the practice attack once more. I asked myself, when will the real attack happen, for which we had practiced so much. This is a new type of adventure, to fight in those desert places. I was certainly bored because of these frequent repetitions. This morning we made the usual business, mostly running and crawling between the sand hills near to the Wady Ghuzzeh. That parade finished at 10 o'clock in the morning and after a cup of tea we had some rest. I wrote several letters to friends at home. In the afternoon I went to Shellal in order to enjoy a bath. What luxury! The second time in three days that I had thoroughly bathed myself; even here in the middle of the desert. Without doubt something will soon happen. The hearsay and gossip grew stronger each day and one believed that we will soon be marching in order to find the Turks. We paraded at 5.30, with our helmets and properties on our back. That life, in which one is able to move easily, undoubtedly presents some attractions. At 6.30 we began to march from the "cactus garden". We marched for two hours in an east-south-east direction across the sand. We made those marches from time to time so that our officers could learn to navigate by compass across the trackless desert. When we finished that march we found that the cooks had already reached the place and already cooked tea and rice for us, which we really enjoyed.

On the following morning, Monday the 1st of October, we woke at 4.30, we ate at 5.30 and began to dig trenches. That task continued until midday, when we waited the arrival of our replacements. We had to stay here until the others came in order to allow us to leave the trenches. We sat there until 3 in the afternoon when the awaited replacements appeared and we happily returned to the camp in order to get something to eat. In the evening we had a conducted communal singing and playing and wrestling between ourselves on the soft sand. Today we received new materials for building our bivouacs; because until now we haven't suitable materials but had to use woollen blankets instead.

We were woken at 4.30 on Tuesday, but didn't get up until the cooks shouted to announce that the meal is ready, because we know that the first parade will not happen until 7 o'clock in the morning. After the breakfast, an inspection of our rifles took place and afterwards our section took care of our machine guns. Afterwards I settled in the bivouac in order to write several letters to home. This day bad news came for our section. We were told that Burnie Binson had to leave our section in order to become a corporal, commanding the machine gun section in the 14a platoon. Understandably we congratulated him on the promotion, but we were very sad because that was the first break in our very happy family circle in more than one year. The remainder of the day we rested because there was no parade.

The following day, Wednesday the 3rd of October, was also free. But the reason for this rest became clear by evening when a midnight parade was announced. At 12.30 in the morning we put the loads on the mules and at 1 o'clock we started marching. We marched by compass until 4.30 in the morning of the 4th of October when at daybreak we were found in the well-known hills of the Wady Ghuzzy. We immediately took part in a practice attack in which our artillery used live munitions. They fired according to the arrangement of a moving barrage, and we followed at a distance of 200 yards behind the forward moving barrage. Afterwards we returned to our camp and set up the bivouacs at 9 o'clock in the morning. But we didn't rest for long and at

10.30 we again started to do practice attacks; and those continued until 5.50 in the evening. We could do some work in the middle of the day because by that time the weather had become somewhat less hot and besides that we are becoming more and more accustomed to the heat.

The morning of Friday 5th October, passed with more of practice attacks until 11 o'clock in the morning. At midday, carrying everything, we paraded and marched back to our home in "cactus garden", which we reached at ten minutes before 4 p.m. And soon we heard something we wholeheartedly hated. We had to parade at 6.30 in the evening in order to exercise ceremonial manoeuvres; there we were in the middle of a sandy desert; we were waiting to attack the Turks; we were already very tired because of practice attacks that day and a march across the sand and after all that were ordered that we make a ceremonial parade!!! But we didn't have time to discuss the matter between ourselves because for three hours the colonel made us march there and back on the firmer sand until we sweated and cursed without interruption. After the parade, before we dispersed, the colonel informed us that our regiment has the honour to represent the Brigade at a general inspection the following morning. That kind of honour was nothing to us then, we were totally dissatisfied about it and what we said about generals in general and ceremonial inspections is not repeatable in a respectable book.

We had to pass that evening by specially cleaning and polishing everything that could be polished for the coming inspection. One pleasing matter was that later some pieces of mail arrived from home. I received three and was made very happy. But to begin with I couldn't read them because it was dark and I didn't have a candle. In a small box I found some grease, and using some tobacco I made a small fire which gave me enough light to read the letters.

Saturday, the 6th of October, began early enough because we were wakened at 3 o'clock in the morning. I ate at 3.30 and paraded at 4.30 for a private inspection. The sergeant inspected us, the lieutenant inspected us, the captain inspected us and finally the colonel inspected us. What a life!

What a war! Finally we marched away to the headquarters of the division where General Allenby inspected us. We, the London Scottish represented the 179a Brigade; the London Irish the 180a Brigade and the 24a London Regiment the 181a Brigade. After the general inspection our divisional general, General O'Shea, spoke to us informally about the coming battles in the new campaign, in order to encourage us to have a courageous and proud attitude. Although we were already accustomed to that kind of address, his words were more pleasing to us because of the informality. He spoke as if he was speaking man to man and not like a superior to an inferior person. Finally we again marched to the camp which we reached at 9 o'clock in the morning. It was announced that we would not parade any more that day, and I passed some time working on letters to be sent home.

There in my diary relating to the Sunday, 7th of October:- "Woken at 5 o'clock in the morning, breakfast at 6 o'clock. Church service at 7 o'clock, afterwards we received some money. Then we knew that in the canteen were many delicious foods – fried eggs – porridge with milk for our evening meal – a very good day.

During the week that followed, we passed monotonously making practice attacks in the Wady.

Sunday the 14th of October, there was a church service when the regimental padre did an interesting talk about "The Origin of the Order of St. John".

On Monday morning a series of football games between the platoons began. Here are the results of the games that took place between the platoons of our company.

Platoon 13 won against Platoon 16 by 2 - 1
  "   15   "   "   " 14 " 2 -1
  "   13   "   "   " 15 " 2 - 1
  "   12 (of Company C) won against Platoon 13
                (of Company D) by 1 – 0

The following day the 19th October, we passed in sporting activities – running, wrestling, mule racing. That evening there was the final game of football, when the Transport Section won 2 – 1 against 'B' company.

Also it was announced that a concert was being arranged and the regimental pioneer section had already erected the stage near the camp. The concert certainly happened the same evening. General O'Shea came in order to listen and the brigade's military personnel came in to order to play various types of music to us. Considering that we were in the middle of the desert, very far from centres of civilisation, the organisers had a good success.

The programme was specially printed for the occasion and the programme was:-

[sf p.144 - 146]

Programme

1. Selection	Brigade Band	Faust
2. Selection	Pipe Band	
3. Overture	Brigade Band	Dutch Kiddies
4. Song	Pte. Hatton	Mountain Lovers Song
5. Song	Pte. Bogie	Where my Caravan has Rested
6. Selection	Brigade Band	Back to Blighty
7. Humorous Scotch Song	Pte.R.McFee	My Old Glengarry
8. Reel	Sgt. Gracie L/cpl. Monsom Piper Stewart Pte. D. Hay	
9. Humorous Item	Pte. Gough	I Love the Army
10. Selection	179th Brigade Quintet	Cavelliera Rusticana
11. L/Cpl Percy Hayden at the piano		
12. Selection	Brigade Band	Carmen
13. Quarrel Scene	L/Cpl Mason and Pte.Brannian	from Julia Caesar
14. Solo	Pte. Milne	One String Fiddle
15. Comic Trio	Ptes. Pearce, Gough, McFee	We're bursting to sing
16. Violin Solo	L/Cpl. Coles	Humouresque
17. Selection	Brigade Band	Songs of Scotland
18. L/Cpl Percy Hayden at the piano		
19. Duet	Ptes. Bogie and D.G. Smith	Watchman what of the Night
20. Humorous Song	Pte. Gough	Cowslip and the cow 21.
21. Two Songs	179th Brigade Quintette	Perfect Day I hear you calling me.
22. Humorous Scotch Song	Pte. McFee	Ten Big Braw Highlanders

The first page of the programme read:-

Programme of Concert Given by Members of 2nd Batt. 14th London Regiment (LONDON SCOTTISH) in the field Lieut. Col. R. L.J. Ogliby, Commandng
----------------- Tuesday, October 16th, 1917 --------------

Several comrades signed my programme because we wished to have a memento of one another in case any from us didn't get through the coming battle [sf p.143 & 145]. When the end of the concert came, the general said some words in order to thank and congratulate the regiment for the successful and enjoyable evening. His attempts weren't very effective because he really drank between some of the programme items. But the intention was clear, and because he was very popular, we heartened him with loud cheers. He was helped into his car and went off happily between hearty hurrahs. And we, having been cheered by the music, recitations and singing, contentedly went to our beds on the desert sand and were soon asleep.

During the days that followed we continued our preparations for the coming adventure. One matter that was very unsatisfactory for our happy family circle, was the arrival of another machine gun for the Platoon No. 15. We were unhappy with this arrival because in a way it caused another break in our family circle. And I, more than the others, was sorry about that because I was the person who was separated from the family. I was promoted and I had to leave my comrades in order to go to No.15 Platoon as the leader of the new machine gun section. Because of this change I was very busy. Firstly I had to inspect the new gun and put in order one or two defects. This is usual with a new gun. Secondly I had to meet my new comrades and arrange about their tasks in the section. Because of the arrival of the new guns, we had to instruct the new marksmen about the gun.

On the 20th of October, I sent the following letter to home.

Dear Dad

    Here are several lines to tell you that I am still well. Recently we have been through an easier time after a period of very intensive exercising and full scale manoeuvring. Now however, in the last three days, I had a lot of work relating to our machine gun. We did that in the morning. In the afternoon and evening football games took place. These were played in order to discover the most skillful player in the Brigade and a fine game took place yesterday. It was a very good and exciting game, between the Trench Mortar Battery and the Machine Gun Corps. When the end of the playing time came each side had scored one goal. Because of that it was decided that they play ten minutes more. So they played ten minutes more and in the final minute the T.M.B, won the deciding point. Our divisional general was present to see the game and at the finish he distributed the prizes. The General O'Shea is a good hearted individual and very popular between his soldiers. He is extremely interested in our well-being and that helps relating to sport and games between us.

    I am sending herewith several pages from my diary, which I have written in the recent months. Also I am enclosing several other interesting things, and please (if they reach you alright) will you save them for me until the end of the War. I am also sending herewith the programme of the regimental concert, took place two or three nights ago. It was an extremely good occasion. Our Pioneer Section constructed a good stage from scrap material. The lighting arrangements were good enough, although they could only find poor lamps. They built the whole thing very skilfully.

    Last evening letters arrived from home. Although almost everyone received some, I didn't have even a letter or paper, and I was extremely disappointed. My companion's letters spoke about the air raids on London.

Did the attacks reach Bowes Park? It is said that the letters mention that bombs had fallen in the northern districts of London. And on account of this and the absence of letters from you I am beginning to fear that something bad has befallen you. It seems to me that nowadays London is becoming as full of dangers as the battlefield itself.

In my opinion, Annie should have some kind of idea about what to do in the event of something bad happening to you. It seems to me that you should prepare a list of information for her about the various things to be done in such an eventuality.

Dear Dad, I don't intent to write so pessimistically, but Annie is quite young and I am a long way from the home land and would not be able to come home very quickly. In fact it is very difficult to get permission to go home from this place in any kind of circumstances.

Now there is not much more to say. I am sending a Serbian coin for David, which is worth two English pence.

Love and greetings to everyone,

Your son

Robin

Editor's Postscript
[Donald Murray]

    Unfortunately the narrative ends on the previous page. From the surviving material it appears that the project was abandoned at that point, however many of the notes from which the document was composed have survived. This collection of papers includes some letters written to family members, from various war zones; and also some drafting notes that effectively constitute a time line of his entire military service. The transcribed timeline is included as an appendix.

Our desert uniform

Robert Murray - October 1917

From the timeline and other various sources, it is known that the battalion fought through Palestine, as part of Allenby's campaign. They were involved in the capture of Jerusalem in December 1917 and subsequent fighting towards the river Jordan. At the end of April 1918, Robert suffered a slight hand wound and was in hospital at Belah for a few weeks, and then suffered a bout of jaundice. In June 1918 Robert returned to his battalion which left the Middle East at end of June to return to France. In July the battalion moved to Eecke, near the Belgium border.

Murray's 1918

Robert enjoyed a spell of home leave during July and rejoined the battalion, which was engaged in fighting in near Eecke. Later on 23rd August he suffered a serious shrapnel wound during the battle for Locrehof Farm (##), after an operation at the 2nd Canadian Stationary Hospital at Outreau, he was returned to England and recovery at the East Leeds War Hospital [A.M.H. Roundhay] near Chapel Allerton in Leeds.

Robert Murray - december 1918

He was demobilised in February 1919 and returned home; and also to his work at the Patent Office. In August 1922 he married his sweetheart, Daisy Forster.

The details of this engagement are not in the main part of the Battalion's War Diary, but referenced in an appendix; that is not included in WO95_2340 (digitised version).

Appendix to RM WW1 Memories
Timeline
[from RM's drafting notes]

1915

29 March	To Watford by train
17 May	Route march to Hatfield. Lord Salisbury's Hse.
18 May	Route march to Ware
19 May	Route march to Bishops Stortford
20 May	Saffron Waldon. Billets & Camp
30 October ?	March to Bishops Stortford. Billets

1916

21 Jan	Train to Warminster. No.9 Camp, Sutton Veney
March	Arrival of first Lewis Gun
24 April	Moved to camp at Longbridge Deverill
28 April	Orders to proceed to Ireland. All except D Company went. Embarked Port Nolloth, Qeenstown; marched to Forty Island. Battn. H.Q. at Tralee.
12 May	Embarked at Rosslare. Fishguard
13 May	Arrived at Warminster
27 May	Inspection by the King
21 June	Entrained for France. Southampton embarked on La Margarite
22 June	Arrived Havre. No.1 Rest Camp
23 June	Entrained Havre Goods Station. Dusk passed Rouen.
24 June	4am. Detrained at Petit Houvin cold drizzling rain.
24 June	Marched to Buneville for rest & beakfast. Reached billets in Averdoingt.
25 June	Marched along St. Pol-Arras road to Marveuil. Billets at midnight.
26 June	Dawn Marveuil shelled. Working party with 185 Tunneling Co. R.E.
6 July	To line for Instruction. 1/7th (Deeside) Gordons
12 July	Took over line. N sector near Neuville St. Vaast
27 July	Battn. To rest at Bray.
4 Aug.	Battn. To line. Relieved C.S.Rifles.
26 Aug,	Battn. To resr at Bray
1 Sept	Battn. Back in line C.S Rifles

4 Sept.	Germans blew a mine almost under our post in Claudot Sap.
13 Sept.	Rest at Bray.
19 Sept.	Back in line. C.S. Rifles. Gerry started to demolish the front line with a new T.M. which threw a bomb weighing 100lbs.
29-30 Sept	Raid on German trenches opposite Paris Redoubt [Heidler 29.12.28]
1 Oct.	Battn. In support.
7 Oct.	Back in line.
13 Oct.	Back to Bray.
20 Oct.	Back in line.
22 Oct.	Relieved by 52nd Canadian Battn.
25 Oct.	Marched to Hermaville
26 Oct.	Marched to Monts-enTernois
27 Oct.	Marched to Fortel
29 Oct	Marched to Montigny-les-Jongleurs
3 Nov.	To Buigny L'Abbé
15 Nov.	Marched to Longpré and entrained for Marseilles
16 Nov.	Midday passed Verailles. Evening food & ablution at Pierelatte
17 Nov.	Dawn reached Marseilles. Musso Camp. [Kronk 31/11/28]
22 Nov.	Marched to Docks embarked on H.M.T Megantic.
23 Nov.	Ship cast off.
26 Nov.	Rough Sea while passing Malta.
28 Nov.	Steaming up Algian Sea, warm weather lovely scenery
29 Nov.	7am. Megantic made fast at Salonica. Dudular Camp.
7 Dec.	Great storm. All tents blown down. [Kronk 10/1/29 see blue paper]
10 Dec.	C. Company embarked at Salonica on "The Wave" & sailed to Vromeri which
11 Dec.	was reached on the 11th midday. Later in the afternoon remainder of Brigade arrived in H.M.S. Endymion & landed from lighters.
12 Dec.	Marched to Katerini on Pelikas river. Long trek 6 days [Kronk 26.2.29]
19 Dec.	Relieved Kensingtons at Pelikas village. Nearby

	was the Mavroneri river.
25 Dec.	Brigade Sports at Katerinu. Only 25% of Batt. Went & remainder had sports near camp.
1917	
5 Jan.	Moved forward to Hani Miljas. "D" Coy. Up on outpost duty. Building of "Chelsea Bridge". Road making. Trench cutting.
13 Feb.	Moved forward to Petra, 1000 feet above sea-level. Went with party taking rations to a French detachment at Kokinopolo via Ajos Dimitrios.
22 Feb.	Marched back to Katerini – 18 miles in 6.3/4 hours with heavy kit through downpour of rain. Not one fell out. [Kronk 3.3.29]
10 March	Left Katerini for the trek to the Doiron front. Reached Tuzla 8 miles (12.8y20
11 March	Marched to Livanovon 13. Bivouaced beside the Vistrica. Sandflies, mosquitoes (02.917)
12 March	To Gida (14 miles) (22.526)
13 March	Topsin Awful roads. (19 miles) (30.471)
14 March	Turned north & followed Vardino to Amatovo (13 miles)
15 March	Halted at Vardino till dusk. Hot day. Reached Karasuli (10miles - 16.09 Km) + (2 miles to camp site) drenched to the skin.
16 March	To Kalinova (15 miles – 25 Km.) Bitterly cold. Snow storm. 9 miles over no roads or bad roads.
18 March	Relieved 11th Scottish Rifles in reserve at Daĉhe. The portion of the line held by the 60th extended from the S.W. spur of the mountainous mass known as the Pip Ridges & ran westwards over the broken hilly country to the Vardar where we joined up with the French. 179th from Whaleback to Little Berkirli. [kronk 8.4.29]
23 March	Bulgar raid Q.W. on Bowls Hill. Everything overlooked by Hill 535. Deserted village of Krastali lay halfway between Bulgar & British lines.
6 April	Bulgars tried a raid but were repulsed by C. Coy patrol.
25 April	Scottish moved to right to Hill 275 & P6. In front were a row of hills which were christened Turtle Back, Pigeon, Single Tree, Tomato & Lancaster.

8 May	Attack on Tomato Hill.
9 May	Continued wiring.
10 May	Relieved by C.S.R. & went into Reserve at Tentre Verte.
21 May	Sudden order to relieve 2.W.R. Nothing doing. [Kronk 17.8.29]
	The Bulgar aeroplane squar- bomb on my post.
7 June	Relieved by 12th Battn Argyle & Sutherlands.
8 June	To Kalinove station. Marched all night to Vergetor.
9 June	To Sarigol.
10 June	To Abarkeni.
11 June	At dawn reached Dudular, passed on to Uchantur.
28 June	Sandstorm & downpour.
30 June	Marched to docks at Salonik. Emberked on H.M.T Aragon.　　　[Kronk 4/9/29] (Describe troopship)
1 July	Put into Mudros. Picked up survivors of a boat torpedoed the previous day.　　[Kronl 27.5.31]
3 July	Disembarked at Alexandria. Trains to Monscar Camp, by Ismailia.　　　[Heidler 6.4.29]
17 July	Marched off through Ismailia into the desert. Followed the canal to El Ferdan.
18 July	To Balah.
19 July	To Kantara
20 July	Bathe in canal. # Day's rest. 9 p.m. entrained for railhead, open ballast trucks with temporary head cover to shade from sun.
21 July	Dawn – El Arish. Bathe in sea. Brekker. 10 am Deir el Belah. Detrained in sandstorm. Camped at Shabasi. Exciting though dangerous bathing.
29 July	March over soft powdery sand to Abu Sitta wells near Shiek Nuran (17 miles).
31 July	Took over from 1/4th Battn. The Welch Regiment in a trench system defending the Wadi Ghuzzi.
26 Aug	Withdraw for special training at El Shauth, known as the Cactus Garden. Night marches to Lone Tree, attack formations at Gamli. Lewis Gun practice at El Ghabi. Continued a HIseia.
2 Oct	First reconnaissance on BeerSheba by officers for making plans.

21 Oct	Left El Shauth. Reached Gambi in afternoon. At dusk carried on to Esani.
28 Oct	Concentrated at Abu Ghalyun, remained to 30th
31 Oct	Battle of BeerSheba.
3 Nov	Left postions taken after battle marched thro B. to Welfare Wadi. Water supply failed owing to sandstorm.
4 Nov	To Welcome Wadi.
6 Nov	Battn. In Reserve to attack on Rushdi & Kauwakah trench systems. Scottish watched battle & bivouced quietly at night.
7 Nov	Moved to a point on the railway line near T. H.Q. to await orders. 4 pm D Coy rush postion at Sheria Wells after 180 Bde had failed all day to dislodge them.
8 Nov	Advance from Sheria driving Johnny through Muntarel el Baghl - took trenches beyond – then saw the charge of the Warwick & Worcester Yeomanry against Austrian & Turkish guns who held on to the end. On run till evening when we halted at the top of a narrow valley at a place called Tor Dimre within three miles of Huj. Two days rest.
11 Nov	Moved to Jemameh via Huj.
13 Nov	Nejilieh eight miles further east. Soccer completion for sheep.
16 Nov	Marched 17 miles to Jindy near Shenia to be as near railhead as possible as transport was the chief trouble in this campaign. All supporting divns. were congregated in various places.
18 Nov	Marched 4 miles to Diah.
19 Nov	Marched to within 3 miles of Gazah.
20 Nov	Mejdel (15 miles) Signs of defeat. T.Ammo train, dead men aminals, abandoned lorries etc.
22 Nov	Junction Station (10 miles) Here the branch to Gaza & BeerSheba left the Jaffa-Jerusalem line
23 Nov	Through Latron to a delightful bivouac ground a Bab el Wadi (14 miles) at the foot of the Judean Hills.
24 Nov	Began ascent of said J.H. Midday Kury at el Enab and during the afternoon reached little hamlet of Beil Nakula. Road making. Sangar building.

8 Dec	Fall of Jerusalem
10 Dec	Outpost fighting on the Nablus Road.
10 Dec	Relieved some of 74th Divn. Near Shafat
11 -12 Dec	Line advanced 1,000 yards.
15 Dec	Relieve by London Irish. In billets in Jerusalem till Xmas Eve. [I went down to a Lewis Gun course at Belah].
24 Dec	Relieved London Irish a Shafat as Battn. In Brigade Reserve. Westminsters & C.S. in line at Ras el Tawil & Tel el Ful.
27 Dec	2 am Turkish Counter attack on Jerusalem.
29 Dec	General advance – 179 Bde. in support.
31 Dec	Scottish Back in Jerusalem.

1918

1 Jan	Relieved 1/6 Batt. Royal Welch Fusiliers on the line Zamby White Hill – Eo Suffa. Marched there via Damascus Gate, across Brook Kedron, up over Mt. Olives, steep path past El Aisawrych village. Weather wet.
9 Jan	Relieved by Q.W.R. – billets on Mt. Olives.
2 Feb	Left this billet where we had a good time. Training road making etc – concerts in Jerusalem in Kaiserin Augusta Victoria Hospice – Route march to Bethlehem at end of period went into canvas.
5 -11 Feb	One long storm.
17 Feb	Moved via Mt. Olives, Bethany, Wadi En Nar for attack on El Muntar.
18 Feb	8 pm commenced advance on El Muntar. Garrison evacuated without struggle.
19 Feb	Evening concentrated at Rujin Rehif
20 Feb	Dashed across to help in attack on Jebel Ekteif. It was all over over when we got there. Travelled via bottom of Wadis all day.
21 Feb	2 am Moved to the attack on Neby Musa (Moses Tomb). Johnny hopped it & we raced the Anzacs Horse in & won. They chased the enemy through Jericho & on to the crossing at Ghoraniyeh.
22 Feb	Manhauling Field Artillery guns down the narrow road into Neby Musa.
23 Feb	Trying march from N.M. 14 miles to Talaat & el Dumm.

24 Feb	March in torrential rain up the famous long steep hill of Bethany to the old camping ground on Mt. Of Olives. 22 in tent.
26 Feb	Marched along Nablus road to Er Ram
27 Feb	Via Jeba, Mukhmas to Ras el Tawil to relieve 2/24 London. Made roads & gradually forward
5 March	the brigade all day among the hills west of Jebel Kuruntal
6 March	B. Coy look for ford over Jordan at Mandesi
7 March	-do- no luck. Left party of six to observe during day. These were seen by Turks & all captured save one. At night the coy. Searched for them of course with no luck.
10 March	C. Coy rejoins Battn. At Kuruntul, from where a tolerable path had been made on to the Jericho plain.
21 March	7 pm moved from Kuruntul on to plain. Reached Wadi Nueiameh & proceeded down to its course to a point three mile from the Jordan.
22 March	2/17 Lond. Tried to force crossing at Ghoraniyeh. Failed. D Coy of ours moved up to support them. 8 am 2/19 Succeeded crossing at Hajlah. Battn. Moved to Wadi Kelt. D Coy. rejoined battn. In early hours of 23.
23 March	Noon. marched to Hajlah & crossed Jordan. Cavalary drove Turks into hills. Scottish reached Ghoraniyeh 9 pm.
24 March	5 am. Moved into shelter in Wadi Nimrin. C Coy. In outpost towards El Hand. 7 am. Moved forward & attacked El Hand, which was captured with prisoner during day. Positions at summit of El Hand all night.
25 March	Dawn Battn. Concentrated joined Brigade & marched to El Salt. Terrible march across poor track. Camped above El Salt.
26 March	Rest in support
27 March	Moved back to El Howey bridge on main road. Delightful biouac. Bathe in Wadi Shaif.
28 March	Returned to El Salt. Rumours of trouble. Halfhearted attack by Johnny. Aussies counter attacked & caned him. 120 prisoners

1 April	Withdrew to Jordan plain.
2 April	Midday recrossed Jordan.
3 April	Rest in bivouacs
4 April	Marched via Jericho to Talaat ed Dum. Bivouaced close to Good Samaritan Inn. Uphill
5 April	Rest
6 April	Uphill to Bethany
7 April	Over Mt. of Olives on to Nablus road nearly to Shafat.
9 April	Marched along Nablus road to Balua Lake – on way to relieve 10th Div.
10 April	Northwards over mountainous country past Jufna to Wadi El Jib
11 April	Scaled north side of this deep gorge and relieved 5th Royal Inniskillings. Spent quiet went seven days.
18 April	Relieved by "Skins"
21 April	Moved south towards Jerusalem by easy stages. (Battn. Was to go over Jordan to attack El Haud)
26 April	Camped at Shafat.
27 April	Long trail down to the Jordan begins again. Bivouacs at Talaat ed Dumm.
28 April	At dusk through Jericho, over river at Ghoraniyeh & reached bivouac area in (29th) Wadi Nimrin at 3 am. (16 miles). No one allowed to move from bivouacs.
30 April	2 am attack on El Haud. About 4 am I was wounded in the hand but carried on & etc.
	Nb. Describe how battle continued. Attack failed.
2 May	Burial Service of killed 33. I back to Jerusalem. Down to Belah - in hospital.
20 May	Eventually to Kantara – Guarding prisoners – Jaundice
2 June	Battn. returns. I rejoin them
15 June	Entrained for Alexandria
16 June	Embarked on S.S. Cambera
18 June	Left Egypt
21 June	Attacked by U boat
22 June	Taranto – wine – bully – drunks –sorehead
25 June	Castellmare – bathe
27 June	Genoa to Cannes, where halted for tea
28 June	Marseilles – Avignon, fire in train we passed in station.

1 July	Reached Audrincq (N.W. of St. Omer (10 or 12 miles). Proceeded at once to Recques. First saw Yanks. From Recques to Serques. Become 30th Div.
8 July	Moved to Eecke. Had halt for night at Ebblinghem and Staple (D.H.Q. Cassel Bde H.Q. St Sylvestre Cappel)
	The Battn. was employed in work on reserve trenches on the south side of the Mont des Cats, where it did much wiring & digging. Reconnoitring for approaches for counter attacks if Jerry broke through. Flêtre, Le Coq de Paille, St Jans Cappel, Nout Farm (near Westourte). In reserve trenches on Mont des Cats on the night a Gerry attack was expected.
2nd half of July	
	Got fortnight's leave. On return helped in breaking down new Lewis Guns.
	During stay at Eecke inspected by Plummer. Saw King George V.
27 July	Relieved 18th H.L.I. The main line was just of Mont Rouge & Mont Vidaigne but the actual front line consisted of very poor trenched overlooked by Mount Kemmel.
3 Aug	To billets at Eecke.
8 Aug	Battn. again in line.
20 Aug	We assembled under the shelter of Mount Rouge & Mont Noir, & after dusk moved down to our jumping off point for the straightening out of the line.
	2.5 am Barrage crashed down. Battle of Locrehof Farm **
Night 22-23	Relieved by C.S. Wounded off to Blighty after operation.
	Calais – Dover – Leeds
	Demobbed Febry 1919.

NB: Further information about his time in Leeds is available from his letters to the family. These are available from the editor either on a CD or via DropBox.

What Not to Wear Under the Kilt

When I received my uniform, many friends in London were very interested, because the Scottish kilt was not often seen in England. One question often asked was whether pants are worn under the kilt.

And that makes me remember an amusing little story about my learning about that matter. Although a son of Scottish parents, on no occasion did I get to know the details of the Scottish national dress. Certainly, I didn't receive any pants among the various clothes given me from the regimental store. So, I sought information from my father who said that, although scots usually didn't wear pants under the kilt, he advised me to do so in London. And he gave me some bright purple pants for this purpose.

One day soon after that, I was doing gymnastic exercises in the regimental drill-hall. We were running around the hall, we ran around many times and from time to time were ordered to lift our knees. Suddenly those accursed pants left their proper place and little by little began to fall. Moving with every step, until finally it appeared around my knees. Several comrades standing nearby saw it and laughed aloud. My neck and face blushed with shame. I had to leave the ranks in order to adjust the garment. Because of that the sergeant severely reprimanded me, adding some hash words about nominal scots who wore those horrible coloured things as an insult to Scottish clothing. My feelings were unprintable and I was very glad when the parade ended and I was able to go home from the mocking jokes of my comrades. That was the last time that pants would be found under my kilt.

Programme of Concert

Given by Members of the 2nd Batt. 14th London Regt.

(LONDON SCOTTISH)

In The Field

Lieut. Col. R. J. L. OGILBY, Commanding

Tuesday, October 16th 1917.

Programme

1. Selection   *Faust*
2. Pipe Band   **Brigade Band**   *Selected*
3. Overture   *Dutch Kiddies*   **179th Brigade Band**
4. Song   Pte. Hatton   *Mountain Lovers*
5. Song   Pte. Bogie   *Where my Caravan has Rested*
6. Selection   **Brigade Band**   *Back to Blighty*
7. Humorous Scotch Song   *My Old Glengarry*   **Pte. R. Mc. Fee**
8. Reel   Sgt. Gracie   L/cpl. Monson   Piper Stewart   Pte. D. Bay
9. Humorous Item   **Pte. Gough**   *I love the Army*
10. Selection   *Cavalleria Rusticana*   **179th Brigade Quintette**
11. L/cpl. Percy Hayden at the Piano

12. Selection   **Brigade Band**   *Carmen*
13. Quarrel Scene   *from Julius Caesar*   L/cpl. Mason & Pte. Brannigan
14. Solo   *One String Fiddle*   Pte. Milne
15. Comic Trio   *We're bursting to Sing*   Ptes. Pearce, Gough, Mc Fee
16. Violin Solo   *Humouresque*   L/cpl Coles
17. Selection   **Brigade Band**   *Songs of Scotland*
18. L/cpl. Percy Hayden at the Piano   *Watchman what of the Night*
19. Duet   **Ptes. Bogie & D. G. Smith**   *Cowslip and the Cow*
20. Humorous Song   **Pte. Gough**
21. Two Songs   *A Perfect Day* / *I hear you calling me*   **179th Brigade Quintette**
22. Humorous Scotch Song   *Ten Big Braw Hielanders*   **Pte. R. Mc. Fee**

GOD SAVE THE KING

Accompanist **Pte. Lyne**

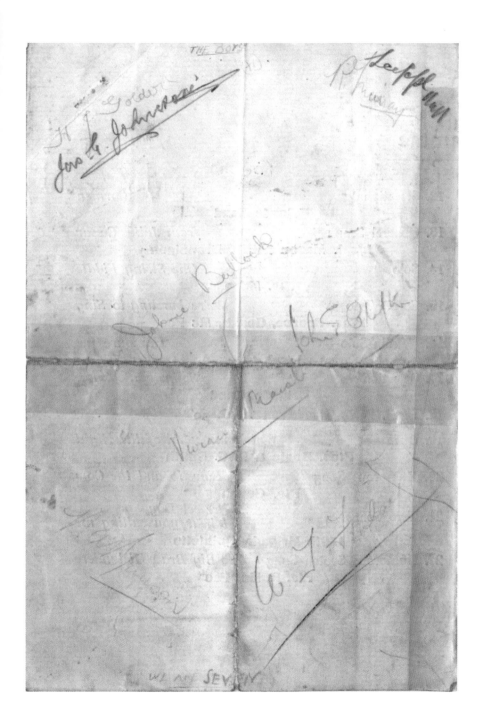

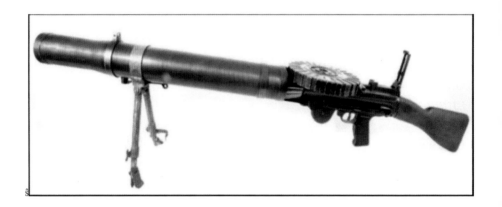

Lewis Light Machine Gun

Printed in Great Britain
by Amazon